AWAKENING FROM THE AMERICAN DREAM

The Human Rights Movement in the United States Assessed During a Crucial Decade, 1960-1970

by
Paul E. Kraemer

C
S
S
R

Center for the Scientific Study of Religion

Chicago, Illinois

This monograph has also been published in Dutch, under the title HET ONTWAKEN UIT DE AMERIKAANSE DROOM, by Uitgeverij Ambo, Bilthoven, 1972.

Printed in the United States of America

Center for the Scientific Study of Religion
5757 University Avenue
Chicago, Illinois 60637

I S B N: 0-913348-04-X

Library of Congress Catalog Card Number: 73 - 78045

TABLE OF CONTENTS

PREFACE v

PART ONE: THE HUMAN RIGHTS MOVEMENT --
WHAT IT IS AND WHY IT IS

Chapter

I. THE MOVEMENT IN THE SIXTIES: A CONVERGENCE OF ROOTS. . . . 3

A New Style Movement 4

Young Radicals as a Case in Point. 5

General Overview: Militancy and the Three "isms". . . . 10

II. THE ROOTS OF THE ROOTS (1): THIRD WORLD REVOLUTION AND URBAN APARTHEID 15

America and De-Colonization--Abroad and at Home. 15

"Two Societies . . . separate and unequal" 19

III. THE ROOTS OF THE ROOTS (2): DILEMMAS OF DEMOCRACY IN "TECHNO-POLITAN" SOCIETY 25

The Movement and the Triple Revolution 25

The Legacy of Total Change 28

Autonomy and Interdependence--Twin Principles in Conflict 34

PART TWO: EMANCIPATION MOVEMENTS --
AN ANATOMICAL INTERLUDE

IV. EMANCIPATION FOR WHAT? A TYPOLOGY AND TENTATIVE CLASSIFICATION. 43

Emancipation Movements as Programmatic Movements 43

Emancipation Movements Sorted. 46

V. AN EMANCIPATION MOVEMENT'S LIFE-CYCLE: A THREE-DIMENSIONAL MODEL 57

The Emancipation Movement in Relation to its Own Components 57

Emancipation Movement Vis-À-Vis the Society and its Response 61

PART THREE: THE MOVEMENT AND THE UNITED STATES -- WHERE ARE THEY HEADING?

VI. FROM "RIGHTS" TO RADICALISM: THE "MOVEMENT" IN TRANSITION 69

From Civil Rights to Human Rights, 1954-1968 69

A First Conclusion: Integration is Dead-- Liberation Instead 75

A Second Conclusion: From Idealism to Ideological Battle 81

VII. TOWARD POLARIZATION--OR WHAT? UNITED STATES SOCIETY AT A CROSSROADS 93

The Not So Silent Majority's Backlash 94

The Vanishing Middle-Ground. 99

The Need of Moving Beyond the Dream 107

APPENDIX 113

PREFACE

This study deals with "the Movement" in the United States, especially during the recent decade of the 1960's. What it attempts to show is that, in this particular period, the one-time movement for civil (that is primarily Negro) rights went through significant changes in momentum, nature, and scope; thus developing into a movement for human rights in the fullest sense. It presented a fundamental challenge to American society in terms of its overall basic ideas, values, and institutions.

Perhaps the strongest urge to write this study was due to the author's keenly felt need to gain a clearer personal perspective about the turbulent social and political events in which he became involved, directly or indirectly, through his work with the Chicago Urban Training Center during the late-1960's. These events could not possibly have left him untouched, neither as a professional sociologist, nor as an individual having his roots in Western Europe (whence he had come, and to where he has since returned). Hence their impact and meaning needed to be sorted out, so that they could be fully grasped and digested.

In a way, therefore, this study may be seen as a personal account by someone who, retrospectively, renders his assessment of the dramatis personae et acta on the American scene at the time of his actual presence there. In this assessment, the central focus is on the movement, its precise nature, and its significance for the critical process of reevaluation so much in evidence in the whole of American society during those years.

However, today, in 1973, there are unmistakable indications of a radical shift of mood. In sharp contrast to the conditions that prevailed at the turn of the decade, the entire nation now seems to be living in an eery climate of non-direction and stunned withdrawal. And as far as the movement is concerned, the conclusion to be drawn is that it has virtually collapsed as a significant force in present-day American society.

How this shift should be interpreted, what it really implies, is by no means clear; least of all to one who, like this writer, has been living on the other side of the Atlantic. Even so, it does raise a rather pertinent question: what relevance can be attributed to an analysis that is largely retrospective in nature, and whose findings apply to a situation that no longer seems current.

Whether or not his findings are relevant is not a matter the author can decide; all he can do is to submit the reasons which prompted him to believe that the results of his labor would be worthy of note, even today.

One such reason is that the current shift of mood does not necessarily imply a reversal of major trends. On the contrary, it is much more likely that these trends persist unabated and in exactly the same manner as they did only a few years ago. Similarly, the great public issues so very much at stake during the 1960's have obviously not been resolved. The underlying conflicts are still there with this difference perhaps: they are now less visibly at work because they have gone below the surface, so that the pressures keep mounting and there is no relief in sight.

In other words, it is fair to assume that the struggle witnessed on the American scene of the 1960's still goes on and will continue to do so in the years to come. And this point leads to a further observation: the ongoing struggle somehow reflects the predicament of the entire Western world in its internal relations as well as in those to the so-called Third World of developing nations. The American experiment may be viewed as the model par excellence of man's Western quest which, as the Dutch historian Jan Romein has observed, has resulted in a decisive break with the general human pattern. It is a break brought about by the rising expectations as well as by the potential fulfillments that have followed in the wake of great revolutions proclaiming man's universal right to dignity and providing the material conditions for the realization of this right. In confronting the movement which envisions a radically transformed life style of truly multiform dimensions to which everyone contributes in accordance with his own unique identity, contemporary America (and with it the entire West) finds itself painfully exposed to the insufficiency of its dream. Having its roots in a basically white-dominated image of man as a primarily rationally oriented being, this dream is now put to the test of a real, all-inclusive universality. The universality of all cultures demands that each be taken seriously on its own terms.

Since this predicament is very much with us, our study may prove helpful in providing a useful perspective for all those existentially involved in it.

January, 1973

PART ONE:

THE HUMAN RIGHTS MOVEMENT --
WHAT IT IS AND WHY IT IS

> In one sense the civil rights move-
> ment in the United States is a special
> American phenomenon . . . But on another
> and more important level, what is
> happening in the United States today
> is a significant part of a world
> development.
>
> Martin Luther King, Jr.[1]

CHAPTER I

THE MOVEMENT IN THE SIXTIES: A CONVERGENCE OF ROOTS

Landing on the shores of the United States in the mid-1960's, the traveler from abroad could not fail to notice a pervasive mood of disquiet and dissent in the society at large. Probably he came somewhat prepared for it through reading his newspapers and knowing, as any right-minded foreigner does, that Americans are a soul-searching lot. Even so, it is likely that he came inadequately prepared in spite of information received by means of mass media and folklore. And who could blame him? Certainly not the natives, who were themselves in large part greatly puzzled at the state of ferment they witnessed in their land.

Yet, four immediate causes of this state were easily identifiable: the race issue, the problem of poverty, the youth rebellion, and Vietnam. But what, in effect, was new about these in the 1960's? The race issue had been part and parcel of American history from the beginning. To be sure, during its history the nation had managed to forget about it as a dominant concern for long periods of time. However, the most recent rekindling of this issue in the national conscience was certainly not something which had occurred overnight. It dated back at least to the 1940's. Similarly, poverty had been a phenomenon familiar to the American scene all along. Perhaps some, particularly among non-Americans, may have entertained the illusion that affluence was a universal condition of postwar America. But many Americans themselves knew better; they knew better either through personal experience or through public denouncements of the "pockets of poverty" which had put the world's richest country to shame even before Michael Harrington's _The Other America_ appeared in 1962. The youth rebellion and Vietnam, on the other hand, were much more recent developments, but by no means entirely novel occurrences. In various forms, such as the leather jackets, juvenile delinquents or beatniks, the revolt of the young had become manifest in the 1950's. And these manifestations had not gone unnoticed, as witness the numerous artistic expressions and/or scholarly investigations that set the older generations worrying and, incidentally, often turned into best-sellers or box-office successes. Also in the 1950's, the nation had become entangled in the troublesome mess of "limited wars" in faraway countries, which proved to be continuous morale-wrecking morasses. To be sure, Vietnam had not yet loomed large at the time, so far as an actual drain on American manpower was concerned. But the initial commitments had been made--to the accompaniment of many a Cassandra-like warning against a woeful repetition of the Korean nightmare of a few years past.

In a word, none of the four factors were entirely non-existent prior to the 1960's. Yet there can be little doubt that these very factors underlay the restive and tumultuous mood that now prevailed. What, then, was new? A plausible answer seems to be that though the factors as such were not new, there was something new in their combined operation. They clearly had become forces that overlapped and interacted, and consequently were cumulative in their effects. This is particularly evident when one focuses attention on that curious multiplicity of social groupings and movements through which those forces found more and more articulate expression in the 1960's, and which increasingly coalesced into the movement.

A New-Style Movement

The movement of the 1960's was unmistakably much more inclusive than, and conspicuously different from, that previously known by this name. In composition and mental makeup, it was a far cry from the "civil rights" movement which traditionally had been equated with the struggle for Negro rights in Caucasian-dominated North America. Its sweep was much broader now, and its goals were more encompassing--even though the plight of the black man in white society still remained very close to the heart of the matter.

This can be demonstrated briefly by reviewing the major elements of this new-style movement, as analyzed and defined by its active participants. When in the late summer of 1967 the Convention on New Politics began its meetings in Chicago--a concerted call to arms of those in radical opposition to established America--at least two leading spokesmen addressed themselves to the question of who the people present or represented were. This they did in position papers prepared for the occasion. That they did not entirely agree on definitions and terms is hardly surprising, especially considering the blunt confession of one of the two: "When we try to examine this question, we reach a vital confusion . . ." Nevertheless, the results of their analytic efforts were strikingly similar, as can be seen by comparing the components identified by each:[2]

I. the Student Movement	I. the Anti-War Movement
II. the Negro Movement	II. the Black Power Movement
III. the Peace Movement	III. the Campus Left Movement
IV. the Liberal-Reform Movement	IV. the Radical Trade Union Movement
V. The Religious Movement (overlapping with III and IV)	V. other movements such as those in the white and Spanish-speaking ghettos, and among the clergy
VI. smaller movements: the "hippies" (especially in their communitarian aspect), the poor whites, the Spanish-speaking peoples, the radical laborites, and (perhaps) the partisans of "new politics"	

Whereas one spokesman (in the left-hand column) considered it questionable to define the "new politics" as a distinct movement, he emphatically voiced the opinion that it should be regarded as the emergent common denominator of all the movements--as the driving principle of the movement:

> . . . before it was even the beginning of a movement itself, the new politics was a form of action and thought for some members of each of the other groups, and a direction of movement for some of them toward each other. It was the leading edge of their approach to society, and the way in which they grappled with the interconnections of the issues that they and people began to see . . .[3]

This notion is significant. It points straight to the essence of what made the movement of the 1960's a new style movement. In the development of this movement, the New Politics Convention of 1967 is a telling landmark. What happened at this convention, or rather what made it important--in spite of its strange proceedings and blatant divisions--was a show of force, bringing together for the first time, in public and on a nationwide scale, the entire range of dissidents who since the beginning of the decade had been mounting their scattered offensives with ever growing fervor. In addition, it signalled, as a matter of record, a definite turn of the tide: away from social appeal and protest, and toward downright political revolt with the sharp cutting edge of civil disobedience and separatism. It marked, in short, the demonstrative rallying cry of the defiant, thoroughly fed up with gradualism and tokenism, and pressing toward radical change NOW!

This shift of mood had made itself felt in each of the component parts, although perhaps to a greater extent in some than in others. It had developed, partly through a process of internal radicalization but probably even more as a result of a process of combustion, sparked by the ever more apparent confluence of currents of dissent and the causes that generated them. This can be illustrated ad libitum--whether one cites the student movement, the peace or anti-war movement, the Negro movement, or any other movement identified above. The mood of fundamental criticism had deepened from a rather subdued but dogged state of protest in the 1950's, to a red-hot determination in the 1960's to dare the powers-that-be. And in that same span of time, each one of these movements had found its own areas of concern and opposition to be more and more intertwined with those of others. As a result, members of different groups could not fail to recognize one another as comrades-in-arms hacking away at the symptoms of sickness they decried in American society and in the world.

Young Radicals as a Case in Point

Take, for instance, that segment of the movement on which a documented report was published in 1966, under the title The New Radicals.[4] The whole matter of the interlacing web of issues and motives is brought home immediately by the publisher's summary of the report. Both report and documents portray analytically what appears in bold capitals on the front (soft) cover: "the young radical activists who have repudiated traditional liberalism and who seek a new vision of America through civil rights, university reform, and anti-war and anti-poverty activities."

This summary, however commercially concocted, is as factually correct as its implications are obvious. The focus is clearly on the young radicals but it is equally clear that their activities cannot be grouped under one neat rubric. The primary context of their activities may be that of the student or campus left movement, but what engages them spills over, cuts across, intersects with the fields of action of almost every other movement cited above. And clearest of all is that these young radicals appear to be dealing with all four root issues--youth, race, poverty and war.

The matter of radicalization also finds expression in the report and its documents. Again, one need only to take a look at the cover, this time the back cover. Here are listed the names of persons and organizations whose activities are discussed: Robert (Moses) Parris, Tom Hayden, Mario Savio, Carl Oglesby, C. Wright Mills, Paul Goodman, Irving Howe, Bayard Rustin, Charles McLaurin, SNCC, SDS, the DuBois Clubs, the Mississippi Freedom Democratic Party, and so on. With a few exceptions, these are names unknown in the 1950's; they represent a brand of radical activism then virtually unheard-of. They signify a "new breed" whose emergence on the public scene had the earmarks of a sudden eruption, occurring around 1960 and gaining in momentum, intensity and scope ever since.

The same fact can be observed again by looking inside the covers of that documented report. Here one finds, among other things, a chronology of events which the authors "selected out of thousands to provide the reader with a rough . . . guide to the development of (this particular segment of) The Movement." Only one page of the 11 pages is needed to deal with the six-year period 1954-1959; but one to two full pages are required for each single year in the equally long period covering 1960-1965. From this simple observation it is clear, once again, that one is confronted with a sequence of events bursting forth with accelerating and accumulating force. However, even more important than the rapid increase in the number of sampled items, especially after 1960, is the change in the nature of these items. As far as domestic events are concerned (these are interspersed with related events abroad), this change is evident in at least three respects:

(a) In examining the actions listed with a view to their immediate initiators, a distinction can be made between three broad categories: "governmental," "private/societal-institutional," and "grass roots." A quick tally shows the following results for the two periods:[5]

Initiators	1954-1959	1960-1965
"governmental"	2	3
"p/s-institutional" (I)		6
"grass roots" (GR)	3	35
combination of I/GR	1	43

The figures and their distributions speak for themselves: since 1960 the initiative passed completely to activists and agencies outside the governmental sphere.

(b) These activists and agencies, surging up from below in a motley assortment, engaged in a burgeoning multitude of moves which show a marked difference in quality as the years progress. This can be seen by examining the types of action in some detail. In the earlier period, the types mentioned include the so-called "beat" literature (with such protagonists as Jack Kerouac and Allen Ginsberg), as well as the first stirrings of student agitation on a few campuses in the Midwest and the Pacific Coast. In the years after 1960, however, there is a rapid proliferation of action, occurring not only on many campuses, but in other locations across the nation as well, and staged by a wide range of individuals and groups. Starting with sit-ins, stand-ins, picketings and freedom rides, these actions soon ran the whole gamut from boycotts, voter-registration drives, vigils, marches and demonstrations of every shade and color, to the formation of committees and community organizations, the issuance of statements and the establishment of national federations and regional political parties of a strongly independent slant; to the support of rent strikes and miners' and farm-workers' attempts at unionization; the organizing of trips to Cuba, summer projects, free speech movements, freedom schools and universities, Mobilizations for Youth and May 2nd movements. To all this must be added the even more dramatic events of traffic blocking, draft-card burning and self-immolation, of campus takeovers, or of black nationalist resurgence (if not insurgency!) and the all-out riots of burn-baby-burn frenzy. In a word, this long list leaves no doubt whatsoever about the rate of radicalization.

(c) At the same time, however, this list suggests the extent to which such actions focused on a steadily increasing variety of issues. To demonstrate this, another tally may be of interest, a tally of the chronological entries taken into account before, but which are now ordered according to the five or six principal topics of concern that kept recurring over the years:

	Topics of Concern	1954-1959	1960-61/	'62-63/	'64-65
1[a]	Youth Protest/Activism	1	1	1	
1[b]	Student Demands/ University Reform	2	1	1	7
2	Peace/Anti-War/ Non-Intervention	1	7	5	14
3	Civil Rights/ Race Segregation	2	6	8	17
4	Independent Politics/ Radical Reform of Society		2	2	6
5	Poverty/Unemployment			5	4
	TOTALS	6	17	22	48

The conclusion is obvious. From this rudimentary statistical analysis, which excludes the many overlappings that in fact abound,[6] it is evident that, especially in the 1960's, the New Radicals had become ever more actively involved in a gradually broadening spectrum of interconnected concerns. The prominence of youth protest and activism (1[a]), spilling over into the campus revolt (1[b]), is hardly surprising in the particular context of predominantly young radicals. Yet the occurrence of the latter development, which escalates from the former, suggests that there is more to it than merely a generational conflict. The nature and intensity of the student agitation, aimed at substantial participation in the administration and reform of educational institutions, indicates that very basic issues are at stake. And this becomes even more evident in the close linkage with the race (3), poverty (5) and peace (2) issues--all questions whose interrelatedness is particularly obvious in the perspective of America's powerful presence in a world divided into white and colored, "have" and "have-not" nations. Indeed, they are all issues which, however distinct, are inseparable in the last analysis, and which, sooner or later, must raise that most fundamental of questions: the adequacy of the existing social and political order, both domestically and internationally (4).

A typical expression of this spectrum of concerns, as underlying the rising tide of a radically inspired rebelliousness in the 1960's, can be found in The Port Huron Statement.[7] This document, issued in 1962 by the then two-year-old "Students for a Democratic Society" (SDS), reflects the agonizing awakening of a new generation to the hollow ring of their society's cherished values in the face of reality. But this is not all; for if it were, this new generation would hardly differ from previous ones experiencing similar disillusionment upon coming of age. What can be heard, in addition, is a sense of great urgency; since the facts--racial bigotry, cold war polarization, nuclear overkill, economic and technological exploitation--are such as to engender the fear that not much time is left to stave off utter chaos and holocaust.

> Not only did tarnish appear on our image of American virtue, not only did disillusion occur when the hypocrisy of American ideals were discovered, but we began to sense that what we had originally seen as the American Golden Age was actually the decline of an era. The worldwide outbreak of revolution against colonialism and imperialism, the entrenchment of totalitarian states, the menace of war, overpopulation, international disorder, supertechnology--these trends were testing the tenacity of our own commitment to democracy and freedom and our abilities to visualize their application to a world in upheaval.

And thus the appeal and search is for a vital change in the basic relations between men and nations, a change guided by a renewed affirmation of man's potential for self-cultivation, self-direction and creativity, and which seeks, as a social system,

> the establishment of a democracy of individual participation, governed by two central aims: that the individual share in those social decisions determining the quality and direction of his life; that society be organized to encourage independence of men and provide the media for their common participation.

Yet this Port Huron Statement is clearly dated. Radical in its wording which speaks of basic changes, it is nevertheless essentially nonradical in its conception of how such changes should come about. It is characteristic of the mood of the early 1960's, when hope was still riding high that the protested wrongs could be righted by appealing to and lining up with the traditional forces of reform.[8] In subsequent years, newly enacted legislation of unmistakable liberal appearance produced little but paper tributes to change-from-within, and for the rest lacked any real enforcement capable of seriously challenging the status quo. In fact, whatever new measures were taken or whatever new policies were publicly pronounced, the result was to adjust rather than transform the existing reality. Thus these measures widened rather than narrowed the gap between those basically committed to the given order, and those who felt or were existentially alienated from that very order. By the middle of the decade, therefore, the process of radicalization was no longer a mere matter of verbal protestations raised to arouse the conscience of men of good will; rather, it had seeped down to the level of action as well. Direct confrontation took the place of persuasion through legally adopted procedures. The building of independent power bases were viewed as the only feasible alternative left when established institutional options for the voicing of dissent failed to respond to the demands for substantial reconstruction. And separatist para- and even counter-formations took shape to undercut the official structures, increasingly felt to be non-committal, if not worse, regarding the core concerns at the grass-root level. In short, a mood of defiance had taken over, bordering on the revolutionary, and scornful of the notion of evolutionary reform.

General Overview: Militancy and the Three "Isms"

What holds true for the so-called New Radicals, is also true of the other major segments of the movement in the 1960's. In one way or another they all showed two interrelated patterns of development. The first was that of a definite growth in militancy. Over the years a distinct trend emerged which, in its most extreme form, resulted in a shift of political positions as sweeping as the swing of a pendulum. No longer was there hopeful reliance on a process of democratic consensus in which every group or interest stood a fair chance to be heard. Instead, one had moved toward a grim collision course with the powers in control, a collision provoked by techniques of "creative disorder," and aiming at a thorough shake-up of the existing system in order to transform it into a new one of a far less constraining nature. This trend was most evident in the quarters of black and anti-war activists whose ranks coalesced to a considerable extent with those of the rebellious students and clergy; to a lesser degree it was manifest in the older movements of leftist radicals of labor and liberal extraction, or the newer ones of white and Spanish-speaking poor.

Parallel with this development, if not underlying it, was a second one: a blurring of issues. Whatever their particular origins, or even their specific concerns, the various groups of oppositionists appeared to be edging together ever more closely, until finally they seemed to have merged into one broad front with two main thrusts. As the years wore on, and especially after the decade's midpoint had passed, there could be little doubt that the foremost foci of contention in the American social and political arena centered around the questions of war and race. This was evident from the haunting prevalence of the Vietnam entanglement and the black intransigence/white backlash polarity in public debates and private minds. Ever since the Watts riots of 1965 and the Senate Foreign Relations Committee hearings of February 1966, these two questions dominated the newspaper headlines, the magazine columns and the broadcast "specials"--with slightly seasonal emphasis on the one during the summer months and on the other during the winter. And most conspicuously, they were the key issues of the long-raging and intensely-waged campaigns of the presidential hopefuls for 1968, dramatically highlighted in President Johnson's withdrawal and the murder of Martin Luther King within the space of four days!

In the view of those constituting the movement, the centrality of these two questions was beyond dispute. Indeed, it found symbolic expression in the widely circulated though abortive attempts at the start of the 1967 New Politics Convention to unite the names of Martin Luther King and Dr. Benjamin Spock on a third party ticket. It was manifest too in the fact that these two men, each of whom was in the limelight as a typical representative of a particular cause, made it unequivocally clear that they were equally committed to the other's cause as well. At the Convention itself, for instance, Spock spoke out not only on the question of war, a matter of obvious concern to him as co-chairman of the National Committee for a Sane Nuclear Policy (SANE); but he also testified to his conviction regarding the issue of the black American's plight:

> The disadvantages which black people suffer in health, education, job competence, employment, have been imposed by the white community through 300 years of abuse and humiliation. The founding fathers declared that people who are oppressed and can find no other redress must rebel. Abraham Lincoln specifically reiterated that right. Black people have long taken oppression ten times as cruel as what the colonists suffered in the 18th century. Whites have practiced a thousand acts of physical and psychological violence on blacks for every act of black violence . . .[9]

King's anti-war position, on the other hand, had become known in speeches and writings dating back to late 1966 or early 1967. It was an uncompromisingly critical one; and the reasons he gave for it were twofold. First, he could not fail to recognize that the struggle for racial equality at the home front was deeply affected by the United States' government's policy of intervention in Vietnam which, especially since 1965, had led to a massive military build-up and consequent reallocation of national resources. Secondly, it was no mere consideration of expedience that made King take his new stand. This position was perfectly consistent with his earlier stand on non-violence as a moral imperative in human conflict. It had made him increasingly aware of the need to arouse the nation's conscience against the war in Vietnam and its constant escalation.

This argument was of special significance, but not because it reflected a generally shared position. Such was certainly not the case. As a matter of fact, particularly among civil rights leaders, there was much disagreement with King's point of view. Moderates feared the estrangement of many in both the white and black communities, whose real or potential support of necessary reforms in the areas of race and poverty might be lost as a result of too close a linking of the Negro cause with the anti-war drive. Far-out militants, on the other hand, scorned such subtleties; to them the relationship was only too obvious. And it made them recklessly push the concept of a full-blown war of color pitting whites against non-whites, not only in the United States but in Vietnam and anywhere else in the world. Yet in spite of all this, King's arguments provided a significant clue. They articulated the fundamental unity which--whether clearly perceived or only incoherently sensed in "gut" fashion--lay at the root of the two issues. This unity rested, as King put it, in the realization that:

> you can't really have freedom without justice, you can't have peace without justice, and you can't have justice without peace; so it is more of a realization of the interrelatedness of racism and militarism and the need to attack both problems rather than leaving one.[10]

In this statement, and especially in the choice of such loaded terms as racism[11] and militarism, the ultimate inextricability of the two main thrusts of the movement of the late 1960's is revealingly expressed. That these major concerns involved more and substantially included the entire spectrum of basic issues raised by all kinds of opposition forces becomes apparent in another "-ism" against which movement spokesmen leveled their barbs. It was again in a phrase of Martin Luther King's that this third "-ism" and its inseparability from the other two, was made explicit. Thus he spoke of the "giant triplet" of racism, militarism and materialism.[12] Others assailed the same unholy triad, either explicitly or by implication--though often with a slight difference in terminology. Usually the word capitalism was substituted for materialism. But whatever the term, the point was clear. Underlying the many diverse movements included in the Movement, there was an acute awareness of an interrelated set of basic ills that cried out for radical change and reevaluation of the existing order and its priorities. Racism showed its renewed rage in the "white backlash," once more laying bare America's--if not the Western world's--age-old schizophrenia; the schizophrenia that consists in championing a civilization dedicated to the rights of man but practicing a systematic exploitation and emasculation of the down-and-out. Militarism, the perennial accomplice of the delusion that might makes right, increasingly exhibited its brutal impact abroad and at home; abroad, in the continuously stepped-up policies of armed-to-the-teeth brinksmanship and crushing intervention, with the prospect of total nuclear annihilation; at home, in the creeping cynicism of a soaring domestic affluence felt to be maintained by the grace of wasteful war procurements, whether that war be hot or cold. Capitalism or materialism, relentlessly pursuing profit, progressively manipulated the market in the interest of giant corporations whose interlockings engulf the earth, thus creating a world where things prevail over people. Alienation became rampant in the face of an increasingly sophisticated technology wedded to the internal logic of economic and political power accumulation rather than working to further social justice and individual self-expression.

In a word, it was in the anguish and anger fomented by these debasing "-isms" that the multifarious strands of recalcitrance found their common bond. And it is this bond that wove these strands together into a passionate commitment to the dignity of man and the worth of his personality.

NOTES AND REFERENCES

Chapter I

1. Martin Luther King, Jr., Where Do We Go From Here: Chaos or Community? (New York: Harper & Row, 1967), p. 169.

2. New Politics Convention. Arthur I. Waskow, "Perspective on '68: Toward a Radical Tammany"; Paul Booth, "New Politics: A Survey and Perspectives," New Politics News (Convention Center of the National Conference for New Politics, Chicago, undated issue).

3. Waskow, New Politics News, p. 5.

4. The New Radicals. A Report with Documents, by Paul Jacobs and Saul Landau (New York: Vintage Books, 1966).

5. The tally does not include all entries but only those relating to the four root issues (race, poverty, youth, peace/war) and actions or measures taken to deal with these issues publicly. Thus, murders, HUAC subpoenas, or Caribbean adventures are excluded; but ensuing reactions of various types are included, together with items like the formation of the Peace Corps, War on Poverty legislation, National Council of Churches projects, SANE-sponsored demonstrations, or student picketings.

6. If recorded, the overlappings would have raised the totals from 6 to 8, for 1954-1959; and from 87 to 143, for 1960-1965.

7. The Port Huron Statement. Jacobs-Landau, New Radicals, pp. 151, 155.

8. Liberal legislation without real implementation, King, Where Do We Go?, esp. pp. 4-12.

9. Dr. Benjamin Spock at New Politics Convention. James Aronson, "The New Politics of Black Power," Monthly Review, October 1967, pp. 13-14.

10. The New York Times, April 2, 1967.

11. One should remember that King's use of this term preceded the Kerner Report (officially: Report of the National Advisory Commission on Civil Disorders, 1968), which turned "white racism" into a current catch-all phrase.

12. Racism-militarism-materialism/capitalism. King, Where Do We Go?, pp. 186 ff. Also Paul E. Kraemer, "The International Youth Revolt," Rebels With a Cause, UTC Pamphlet No. 1 (Chicago: The Urban Training Center, 1967), pp. 11-12.

CHAPTER II

THE ROOTS OF THE ROOTS (1):

THIRD WORLD REVOLUTION AND URBAN APARTHEID

An understanding of the essential oneness of the movement and its root concerns is important. But it is not enough. At least two other questions need to be touched upon: a somewhat fuller appreciation of the roots of the roots; of the wider context out of which the major motives emerge and receive their drive; and then one must ask what in this context seems to have contributed to that special note of urgency so characteristic of the movement in the 1960's.

Historians, social philosophers and others, together with their popularizers, have long been successful in finding acceptance for the idea that World War I marked the abrupt end of a specific era in modern history. It plunged civilized mankind--a Europe-centered mankind revelling in *la belle époque* of *fin de siècle* progress--into the ghastly convulsions out of which a new era was born. It is obvious, however, that the birth pangs, begun with the ferocious barrage of "the guns of August" (1914), did not reach their horrendous climax until more than 30 years later, in the atomic incineration of Hiroshima and Nagasaki (August 1945). It was only then, after that final World War II act of terror, that the new era began to show its first, clearly discernible contours. But even at that time the full import of what had been shaken loose in three decades of bloodshed and upheaval could hardly be perceived. The post-1945 world witnessed an almost completely revolutionized order--politically and socially, economically and technologically, and perhaps above all psychically. Yet the actual scope and intensity of this revolution did not dawn till at least another decade had passed, since it was simply too big with the seeds of change *per se*.

America and De-Colonization--Abroad and At Home

Most immediately evident was the eclipse of the old, Europe-dominated power constellation. An entirely new constellation had emerged, with two superpowers, the United States and the Soviet Union, vying with each other in a steadily widening battle for the allegiance of a rapidly rising third force. In particular this third force, made up of the continuously swelling ranks of the independent nations of Asia and Africa,[1] became a key factor in the developments that unfolded in the aftermath of World War II. Not only their vast increase in numbers, but even more their common past as victims of colonialism, bound these nations together in a strong sense of solidarity. Anti-colonialism united them, but soon this mood took on anti-white overtones. And in this process the United States became entangled in a very special way; for there was the unmistakable fact to which Harold R. Isaacs has called attention:

> The downfall of the white-supremacy system in the rest of the world made its survival in the United States suddenly and painfully conspicuous. It became our most exposed feature and in the swift unfolding of the world's affairs, our most vulnerable weakness.[2]

Initially perhaps, this fact was somewhat shrouded. In the immediate post-war period, the United States' active role in promoting de-colonization in accordance with its anti-colonial tradition tended to make its supremacy in world politics rather an appealing asset, obscuring the liability of its whiteness. But in subsequent years, Isaac's observation proved only too true. This was partly the result of the rush of events in the outside world, which forced America into a position of championing instead of challenging the status quo. First, there was a tightening of the cold war and a consequent rapprochement with the colonial powers of old. Then, there was the indomitable surge of nationalism in the strategically vital areas of South East Asia and Africa, a surge which left those very colonial powers no choice but to succumb, willingly or unwillingly, and sometimes without any will at all. The United States was caught in the middle of two equally pressing necessities: to fill the void and to make its peace with the new states. And eventually there was the gradual disintegration of the once solid power blocs, a development which pushed the United States--so historically impregnated with anti-Communism intensified by cold war conditions--toward a course of going it alone on the slippery tightrope of dominant leadership in a freedom-hungry world. Thus, step by step, this country found itself more clearly identified as the heir apparent to the white man's burden. It was faced with the task of salvaging the insolvent remains of colonialism vis-à-vis a host of creditors suspicious of the least sign of alleged, or real, neo-colonialism.[3]

This was not all, however. Parallel with and greatly stimulated by these happenings abroad, a long-smouldering domestic crisis burst into flame and, thereby assumed entirely new dimensions. The impact which World War II had on the United States as a whole--namely that of putting it at the center of world politics--inevitably affected the position of its black community as well. Even during the war itself this was evident to Gunnar Myrdal who, in his famous study of America's racial problem, spoke of "tremendous international implications."[4] He placed prime emphasis on the end of this country's isolation and its emergence as a prominent force in the global struggle waged in the name of freedom and democracy. This necessitated, for reasons of international prestige and trustworthiness, "a redefinition of the Negro's status in American democracy." In addition, he pointed to "the color angle to this War," but as a minor factor--"at least . . . in the short-range view"; for in his opinion, the black American was "thoroughly American in his culture and whole outlook on the world," even though there could be no doubt as to "some vague feelings of solidarity and allegiance to the cause of other colored people involved in the world conflagration."

Special note should be taken of these two implications, as foreseen by Myrdal. For as a matter of fact, both are precisely the ones that in following decades would play a decisive part in bringing the American racial crisis to a head--albeit in a gradually reversed order of importance. The redefinition of the black American's status became indeed a crucial issue in and for a nation which had to assume international leadership in a world in which the new Asian and African states' emergence from colonialism constituted the great challenge. In such a world, the fundamental test of the United States' commitment to the principle of democratic self-determination was not merely a matter of astute diplomatic rhetoric backed by consistent foreign policy moves, but depended as much on the country's domestic performance in breaking with long-entrenched discriminatory practices.

The implication of this was certainly not lost on those in high positions in the United States government. Unbelievable as it may seem in retrospect, the first formal step since Reconstruction to correct inequalities based on race was President Roosevelt's executive order of 1941, banning discrimination in defense projects and establishing the (temporary) Fair Employment Practices Commission. This order represented the most important accomplishment of the entire New Deal period in the field of civil rights, otherwise so actively devoted to the furthering of social democracy. And what is more, it was issued only with great reluctance and under severe pressure from black organizations threatening to stage a march on Washington. Remembering this, it is only fair to say that the post-1945 record bears ample witness to a true change of climate in America's handling of the race question, especially by the federal government. In 1948, President Truman, by no means a northern liberal, ordered an end to segregation in the armed forces and firmly supported attempts to initiate a comprehensive legislative program for civil rights. In 1954, the United States Supreme Court overthrew the "separate but equal" ruling of 1896, and decreed that integration of public schools be undertaken "with all deliberate speed." In 1957, again under the aegis of the conservative Eisenhower administration, Congress approved the Civil Rights Act--a feat unrepeated in its annals since the 1870's, but which it now soon followed with a second, somewhat strengthened, statute in 1960. The momentum continued in the Kennedy-Johnson years, with such important examples as the 1961 ruling by the Interstate Commerce Commission that rail and bus terminals might not be segregated; the executive orders of 1961 and 1963 reenforcing nondiscrimination in both government and private employment involving federal contracts; the Civil Rights Act of 1964, which black leaders hailed as "a giant step forward" (Roy C. Wilkins), or at least as bringing "a cool and serene breeze to an already hot summer" (M. L. King); the Voting Rights Act of 1965, specifically dealing with the hard core problem of unequal registration procedures and other practices aimed at denying the ballot to black voters; and finally, the so-called Fair Housing Act of 1968, rushed into passage following the assassination of Martin Luther King.[5]

Yet all these indications of progress, however impressive if compared to the staggering inactivity of the preceding three quarters of a century, were like crumbs to the starved. They were too little, too insubstantial; hence they strained rather than eased the relations between the races. Their net effect was to whet the appetite of the long underfed, whose apparent gluttony in turn was bound to cause reservations, if not worse, among their "benefactors" (which, after all, is a well-known socio-psychological chain reaction in interpersonal as well as in intergroup behavior).

But this progress was not only too little; above all it was too late. For in the meantime a fundamental change had occurred in the minds and attitudes of the dependent as they began to raise a number of basic questions about the nature of their dependency. One such question was the one to which Gunnar Myrdal alluded when mentioning "the color angle." While white America busied itself with the chores of free world leadership abroad, and stumblingly tried to match this with the Fair Deal through the Great Society at home, the black American had ample occasion to develop less and less "vague feelings" as to his "solidarity and allegiance to the cause of other colored peoples." This process had, from the perspective of its primary subject, both positive and negative aspects. But to the large majority of whites who saw it take shape in their midst, without being able to control or even understand it, it could only become threatening and deeply disconcerting--thus setting in motion a vicious circle of reciprocal alienation that affected everyone.

Viewed positively, the black man in the United States gained a new self-awareness from the rebirth of Asian and African nationalism with its attendant acquisition of political independence. In this post-war development, there was much more at stake than the need for America's white majority to grant equal citizenship to its black minority for the sake of credibility in a decolonizing world. Of far greater importance was the psychological and cultural impact on the American black man as a man of "color." At long last he could identify with a past that was his own, not disconnected and deformed, but rooted in a proudly rediscovered heritage of richly diversified traditions. No longer was he condemned to live in a vacuum that deprived him of any personal or social self-affirmation, save as an outcast desperately trying to find his niche in a totally alien environment. Now his stigma, which he had never been allowed to cast off or forget, became his passport to the stirring, worldwide community of "soul" that, in revolutionary temper, affirmed its determination to ride the wave of the future. Instead of being a displaced nonentity, neither slave nor free, he found himself a participant in the sweeping movement which had as its objective--in the words of Chief S. O. Adebo, of Nigeria: "to restore to the man of color, wherever he may be, whether in Nigeria, or in the United States, or in Moscow, or in Brazil, the dignity of a human being."[6]

Negatively, of course, this meant a break--with the black American's Americanness in culture and outlook. There cannot be the slightest doubt that this was a highly unsettling experience that increased his awareness of the marginality that had always been his. The three hundred years he had spent in dogged attempts to strike roots--however subculturally--in American soil, could not be erased by a mere act of will. They had necessarily resulted in an existential attachment to a way of life and thought which, in spite of everything, held sway over his allegiance, the more so as this way of life and thought had offered occasional glimpses of near-fulfillment. To unshackle himself from such attachment and embark on a reorientation of his identity could not but rend him apart, torn between two loyalties. It is hardly surprising, therefore, that in his efforts to find a new integrity, a whirl of clashing emotions sought an outlet in a wide (if not wild) variety of expressions and counterexpressions. "Integrationism" vied with "black power" advocacy, "reconstruction" with "black revolution," redefinition of the black man's cultural self-image as Afro-American with the total rejection of anything but self-supporting, secessionist Africanism. Caught in an internal split of agonizing magnitude, his position as a whole toward American society shifted away from that society. Inch by inch, as it were, his disaffection grew and became more manifest. This was largely the result of a number of forces operative on the American domestic scene for many decades, but recently producing effects that were both unprecedented and unexpected.

"Two societies . . . separate and unequal"

It seems to be a (tragic) irony of fate that the forces in question are precisely the ones that had in previous years led many observers to strike a note of optimism regarding the future of race relations in the United States. Among these observers was Gunnar Myrdal. In his *An American Dilemma*, published in 1944, he pointed to "the great migration to the urban North" as the powerful development which caused the Negro problem at that time to become increasingly national in scope. No longer was this mainly a southern problem; the north now became involved, too, and this spelled a definite change toward greater equality in the long run. For it was Myrdal's (and others') strong conviction that the large-scale black exodus to the north meant the emergence of a political element which--in coalition with other reform-minded voting blocs such as labor--would eventually be of sufficient weight to check southern conservatism and force the north to let liberalism prevail in the interest of both national progress and international prestige. It is beyond dispute that, in the years after World War II, these expectations seemed to be corroborated by the actual events. As indicated before, America's black minority took many "a giant step forward" indeed on the road to full citizenship. Yet at the same time, the very forces that had set this process in motion, appeared to have something entirely different in store as well: a massive *de facto* apartheid which prompted Gunnar Myrdal (in 1967) to draw poignant parallels between the situation in the United States and the Republic of South Africa.[7] Or to put it in terms of the basic conclusion at which the Kerner Commission on Civil Disorders arrived in 1968: "Our nation is moving toward two societies, one black, one white--separate and unequal."[8]

De-agraranism, industrialization, and urbanization, in the final analysis, appeared to be culminating in a segregation along color lines that defied all categories of imagination in a nation wont to bank on the morality of the common man's common sense as the prime mover of pragmatic idealism-at-work. In the 1960's, this harsh reality began to dawn in the wake of a painful encounter with the urban crisis. Not only did America find itself faced with the perplexing complexity of the metropolis as the dominant social milieu--a milieu seriously at odds with the nation's traditional predilection for localism, its aversion to centralization. But also America was rudely awakened to the accumulation of social disruptiveness that definitely accompanied the urban sprawl. The symptoms became manifest in all shapes and manners: inner city blight, surging crime, crushing problems of traffic congestion, water and air pollution, dwindling tax bases, deteriorating public services, disorganization and fragmentation of governmental resources and administrative controls. Above all, such symptoms appeared in the almost complete disintegration of intra- and inter-communal relations, resulting in an amassing of "social dynamite" ready to go off on the slightest provocation. Rochester, N. Y., Harlem, and Brooklyn, in 1963 and 1964, might at the time have been regarded as isolated incidents. But soon it became evident that they only marked the beginning of a cataclysm of explosions that summer after summer rocked scores of cities all across the nation. Watts, Newark, Detroit and Washington stand as grisly monuments. What had gone unnoticed for years amidst the rush and tumble of a busily forward-pushing nation, now suddenly burst into the open.

In 1950, roughly half of the United States population lived in metropolitan areas (over against slightly less than one-third in 1900). In 1960 this amounted to more than three-fifths; in 1968 close to two-thirds. But these figures tell only part of the story. The rate of change was vastly different for white and black Americans: between 1950 and 1968 the number of black metropolis dwellers grew more than twice as fast as that of white ones. Even more significant, however, was the difference in the direction of the two flows. Whites moved steadily to the metropolitan outskirts, blacks to the core cities, with the result that, between 1960 and 1968, the white population of the large urban centers decreased by 1.7 million (or -3.6 per cent); whereas the black population increased by 2.1 million (or +21.6 per cent). Over the same period, whites increased by 13.2 million in the urban fringe; blacks by about 600,000.[9]

Spelling this out in terms of the developments in one major metropolitan center--Chicago--it meant a doubling of the black population: from one half million in 1950, to over one million in 1967. It also meant a continuous expansion of "black territory," from "five smaller islands interspersed among white neighborhoods" in 1950, to two vast areas on Chicago's south and west sides, together comprising 39 square miles, where:

> --a man can walk ten miles almost in a straight line, and never pass a home occupied by whites;
> --housing conditions are three times more substandard and five times more dilapidated than in the city's white communities (yet with median rents exactly identical to the ones paid by inhabitants of the latter, to wit $86 per month);
> --personal income lags increasingly behind that of the average white Chicagoan, showing a widening gap since 1950, so that by the end of 1967 the ratio was in the order of 1 to 2;
> --people are four times as likely to be out of work, one-half as likely to have a skilled craft, and even if they are college graduates, "earn less than white, high school dropouts."[10]

Metropolitan America of the 1960's had become a landscape of shocking contrasts. Amidst the spreading lustre of prestigiously rebuilt downtown districts and profusely catered-to suburbias, where the good life came within reach of ever broader segments of the people, desolate blots of decay and deprivation not so slowly and surely ate their way into the central cities. Here in these central cities, once the free ports-of-entry for millions in search of a new future which would (and eventually did) enable them to move on as they pleased, other millions now found themselves locked in inescapable ghettos. Black ghettos in a white man's land--politically sealed off from the seats of power and the conspicuously abundant emoluments derivable therefrom; economically lacking the skills and resources to compete in a highly specialized, technologically geared market, controlled by financially supersized interests; educationally victimized by wretchedly inadequate facilities, overcrowded, understaffed, non-motivated, from which to drop out makes often as much or little sense as to graduate, since there is no place to go anyway; culturally mutilated for want of an environment with which to identify, other than that of the stereotyped non-man whose sole recourse is the dogged will to survive; socially despised and stigmatized, discriminated against and physically pushed out of sight in a no-man's-land of squalor and unending frustration, where the outside world is encountered only in the hateful representatives of high-handed law and order, absentee-ownership exploitation and degrading "welfare colonialism."[11] These are ghettos, compulsory in the fullest sense--though legally non-existent; compounds of outcasts, whose state of institutionalized exclusion is an anachronism set in the midst of a society that promises, and to a considerable extent ensures, prosperity and participation to all.[12]

A chasm of staggering dimensions split the metropolitan milieu into two, entirely separated and fully estranged worlds. On the one side was the world of the increasingly affluent beneficiaries of the American-Dream-Come-True; a world eagerly reaping the fruits of society's opportunities while turning its back on the wasteland it creates in the process. On the other side was the world of those trapped in a down-spiral of unfilfilled hopes, blocked ambitions, denied or simply non-existent possibilities; a world without means of its own, but living at the mercy of reluctantly provided hand-outs, and for the rest, left to itself in a jungle of mounting apathy, despair . . . and radicalized anger.

Confronted with this chasm on the home front, yet acutely aware of a world scene where colored nations joined in a revolution of rising expectations, America's black men had little choice but to revolt. This revolt found an outlet in escalating violence, either individually staged through crime, or massively exploding in riots. It found an outlet as well in the soaring sentiments of "black consciousness." These sentiments took many forms, ranging from expressions of self-affirmation such as "black nationhood" or "black Christianity," to cravings for self-assertion by means of "black power" and "black liberation." But they had one thing in common: they were evidence of an open conflict with white-dominated, American society. "Integration" was spurned as a sham and a fraud characteristic of the white colonialist's bag of tricks.[13]

NOTES AND REFERENCES

Chapter II

1. Excluding South Africa and Israel as typically non-indigenous, the number of United Nations members from the Middle East, Asia and Africa, increased from 12 in 1945 to over 70 in 1970. This represented a growth from 23 to close to 56 per cent of the total United Nations membership, which over that period soared from 51 to more than 130.

2. Harold R. Isaacs, The New World of Negro Americans (New York: Viking Press, 1965), pp. 6-7.

3. Race issue in World War II aftermath, Isaacs, New World; Rupert Emerson & Martin Kilson, "The American Dilemma in a Changing World: the Rise of Africa and the Negro American," Daedalus, Fall 1965, pp. 1055-1106; Harold Cruse, The Crisis of the Negro Intellectual (New York: William Morrow & Company, 1967), esp. pp. 420 f.

4. Gunnar Myrdal, An American Dilemma (New York: McGraw-Hill Book Co., 1964), Vol. II, pp. 1015-1016.

5. U.S. Government actions on civil rights, Myrdal, American Dilemma, Vol. I, pp. xxxiii-xxxiv; Arthur M. Schlesinger, Jr., A Thousand Days (New York: Fawcett Crest Book, 1967), pp. 844 f.; The Negro Handbook (Chicago: Johnson Publishing Co., 1966), sections III, V, VII-IX.

6. Chief Adebo. Emerson-Kilson, Daedalus, Fall 1965, p. 1080--quoting from a speech by Nigeria's representative to the United Nations, addressed to the American Negro Leadership Conference, September 29, 1964.

7. Myrdal on "The Great Migration to the Urban North," American Dilemma, Vol. II, pp. 1010 f. On apartheid in the U.S., in a late-1967 interview reported in American newspapers.

8. Report of the National Advisory Commission on Civil Disorders (New York: Bantam Book, 1968), p. 1.

9. Bureau of Labor Statistics & Bureau of the Census, Recent Trends in Social and Economic Conditions of Negroes in the United States (Washington, D.C.: U.S. Government Printing Office, July 1968), p. 4.

10. Chicago data. Ben H. Bagdikian, "The Black Immigrants," The Saturday Evening Post, July 15, 1967; Chicago's Widening Color Gap, by Pierre de Vise (Chicago: Interuniversity Social Research Committee Report No. 2, December 1967), p. 88.

11. "Welfare colonialism," Charles E. Silberman, Crisis in Black and White (New York: Random House, 1964), p. 313. An apt (self) description of "welfare colonialism" was given in a 1962 policy statement by the then Director of the Cook County (Chicago) Department of Public Aid: "This group (the welfare recipients) understands less and less of what is expected of it and how it can go about fulfilling its duties and responsibilities, just as those who wish to help them find it more and more difficult to communicate with them and to know about helping them. But at such a point, society can no longer accept the passive role of mere support; it must begin to lead and direct the individual . . . Just as the child is expected to attend classes, so also the 'child-adult' must be expected to meet his responsibility to the community. In short, 'social uplifting'--even if begun on the adult level--cannot expect to meet with success unless it is combined with a certain amount of 'social disciplining'--just as it is on the pre-adult level." Thus it was urged that relief recipients should be forced to go to school, on penalty of losing their welfare benefits.

12. Ghettos as compulsory institutions, Louis Wirth, The Ghetto (Chicago: Phoenix Books, 1966), ch. III.

13. Black consciousness and revolt. Illuminating descriptions and expressions of "the black condition" and its effects on the shaping of individuals' lives as well as societal events: The Autobiography of Malcolm X (New York: Grove Press, 1966); Albert B. Cleage, The Black Messiah (New York: Sheed and Ward, 1968); Eldridge Cleaver, Soul on Ice (New York: McGraw-Hill, 1968); Robert Conot, Rivers of Blood, Years of Darkness (New York: Bantam Books, 1967); J. Archie Hargraves, "Not What Makes Sammy Run--But What He Does Now to Ensure His Future and Reclaim His Past," You'd Better Listen, Mr. Charlie, UTC Pamphlet No. 2 (Chicago: The Urban Training Center, 1968), pp. 21-35.

CHAPTER III

THE ROOTS OF THE ROOTS (2):

DILEMMAS OF DEMOCRACY IN "TECHNO-POLITAN" SOCIETY

The "color revolution" is not an isolated phenomenon. It is but one aspect of the process of change per se that had become the order of the post-1945 world--a most acute aspect, to be sure, yet essentially a manifestation of the same crucial questions that were being increasingly raised since the 1960's by various other movements of revolt.

The Movement and the Triple Revolution

It is no mere coincidence that the scope of the movement which developed on the American domestic scene, had widened. From a movement concerned about Negro civil rights it grew into a groundswell of rebellion against racism, militarism and capitalism/materialism. In fact, there was an inner logic to this development that reflected the vast and rapidly accelerating changes which by mutual reinforcement, shook the foundations of the entire societal order, both national and global.

What the movement demonstrated on its own level found expression on another level in the memorandum which was made public in March 1964 by The Ad Hoc Committee on The Triple Revolution.[1] In this memorandum, addressed to the President of the United States, a widely diversified group of influential men and women urgently called attention to three separate, but simultaneously occurring and interacting, revolutions:

> The Cybernation Revolution: A new era of production has begun. Its principles of organization are as different from those of the industrial era as those of the industrial era were different from the agricultural. The cybernation revolution has been brought about by the combination of the computer and the automated self-regulating machine . . .
>
> The Weaponry Revolution: New forms of weaponry have been developed which cannot win wars but which can obliterate civilization. We are recognizing only now that the great weapons have eliminated war as a method for resolving international conflicts. The ever-present threat of total destruction is tempered by the knowledge of the final futility of war . . .
>
> The Human Rights Revolution: A universal demand for full human rights is now clearly evident. It continues to be demonstrated

in the civil rights movement within the United States. But this is only the local manifestation of a worldwide movement toward the establishment of social and political regimes in which every individual will feel valued and none will feel rejected on account of his race.

This triple revolution, as defined by a select group of persons whose high standing with the establishment was beyond question, bears a striking similarity to the three "-isms" against which the movement registered its angry opposition. The terms may differ but the areas of concern appear remarkably parallel. Moreover, not only in subject matter did the movement and the Ad Hoc Committee show a large measure of agreement, but also in their sense of urgency. The note of radicalism, so characteristic of the movement's evolution since the early 1960's, also reverberates in the Committee's emphatic references to the threat of "unprecedented economic and social disorder" and "the necessity for radical alterations in attitude and policy."

In other words, it is obvious that the movement's passionate dissent could not be disregarded as mere hot-headed rhetoric feeding on itself. On the contrary, it was an awareness of the significance of recent developments that led such reputable men and women as made up the Ad Hoc Committee to confess to "a feeling of foreboding" and "the recognition that mankind is at a historic conjuncture which demands a fundamental reexamination of existing values and institutions."

This last quotation emphasizes yet another important point. Like the movement, the Committee viewed the changes that were going on around them as having truly historic and worldwide significance. The issues at stake were not merely internal and national; they involved the entire world and revealed a global civilization caught in the dilemmas of its own exploits. That is, a civilization swept by marvels of technological genius and teeming with highpowered ideals of universal freedom and equality, yet thrown in disarray by their staggering consequences. It was the civilization of one world whose inhabitants were woven together in inescapable interdependence, yet at the same time strove for the fullest measure of autonomy. It was the civilization of "Technopolis"--to use Harvey Cox's apt neologism--where the accomplishments of the scientific revolution had set the stage for the all-inclusive community of men whose fate hinges on each individual's ability to share fully in shaping the res publica, the common cause of all fellow-men.[2]

In the perspective of this global, technopolitan society, the movement within the United States was but a local manifestation indeed. It was a local manifestation of a surging tide, enveloping all continents, and challenging with revolutionary fervor the prevailing patterns of power distribution and value orientation. Of this tide, the struggle against white racism and black deprivation in America's metropolises was as much a part as the fight for dignity and nationhood of the colored peoples engaged in the process of decolonization; the ban-the-bomb and anti-war protestations were as much a part of it as the new generation revolt, apparent on either side of the Atlantic, and decrying the rigidly institutionalized establishment, with its emphasis on success, on profits, and on benign officials.

Some of the factors that precipitated this worldwide wave of refusal to go along have already been pointed out. They were embodied in the coincidence of two developments that, particularly in the 1960's, deeply affected the United States both domestically and in its relation to the outside world. On the one hand, there was the urban crisis; on the other, the increasing evidence of the post-war world's true division: not a clean-cut dichotomy between a communist East and capitalist West, but a widening gap between the abundantly rich superpowers to the north and the desperately poor, technologically outpaced nations to the south. This division proved even more acute because it ran along color lines thus infusing into an economic conflict of almost insurmountable dimensions an even more perilous one of racial, if not racist, controversies.

However, these factors alone cannot be considered sufficient explanation. They do not account for the rebelliousness equally manifest in countries which--in sharp contrast to the United States--were hardly, or at least incomparably less, exposed to urban crisis at home and political entanglement abroad. Take for instance the case of the Netherlands. Whatever its problems--due to internal or external conditions requiring major readjustments, especially after World War II--by about 1960 this country could certainly be regarded as a show-case of urban and regional planning, social and economic democracy, and political stability. Unperturbed by color predicaments, and--like most of the nation-states of post-war Western Europe--unburdened by the immediate stress of big power responsibilities, it was in the privileged position of being able to focus primarily on domestic reform policies.[3] Yet the Netherlands witnessed no less a spirit of revolt and recalcitrance which in the 1960's appeared to be spreading like wildfire around the globe. In 1966 and 1967, particularly, the Netherlands was the scene of a curious movement of youthful *agents provocateurs* whose fierce but short-lived spree of hell-raising, leg-pulling and reputation-flouting turned out to be but a mild prelude to the students' explosions of 1968 and after elsewhere in Europe (Paris, Berlin, Amsterdam). These "Provos," as they became known, dedicated themselves to the following principles:

> *Provo* has something against capitalism, communism, fascism, bureaucracy, militarism, snobism, professionalism, dogmatism and authoritarianism;
> *Provo* finds itself put to the choice: desperate resistance or meek submission to the crack of doom;
> *Provo* appeals to rebels with or without a cause to put up a fight wherever they see fit;
> *Provo* realizes that ultimately it will be the loser, but it is not going to miss the opportunity of at least once provoking this society to its very core.[4]

In other words, more must be involved; and in fact, this "more" is directly implied in the first of the Provo principles. Here one finds a clear indication of another division--less easily discernible than the one mentioned earlier, but probably of even greater significance. It is a division which again involves the obsolescence of old dichotomies and their replacement by the newly emerging lines of demarcation in today's world. This time, however, the shift that became manifest was no longer a growing gap between societies at different levels of development, but rather had its locus specifically in the highest developed societies, and evolved from the very forces that caused these societies to arrive at their advanced stage.

The Legacy of Total Change

The forces in question are the ones which appeared in the late-eighteenth and early-nineteenth century and set in motion a total revamping of conditions, institutions and ideas. In a word, they can be subsumed under the general headings of the French and the Industrial Revolutions--that is, that powerful complex of interacting processes which thoroughly altered man's relationship to his material and social environment and which continue to do so at an ever-accelerating pace. Under their impact, modern Western civilization entered an era of unprecedented creativeness regarding the subjection of nature and the organization of society. The salient features of this era are perhaps most conspicuously the parallel phenomena of a veritable explosion in science and technology and the rise of industrialized "mass" democracies enjoying heretofore unsurpassed possibilities for political freedom and economic growth. Yet these extraordinary accomplishments entail equally extraordinary implications, which underlay the turmoil of the 1960's, when a whole new breed of radical protesters came to the fore, most noticeably among the younger generation.

The profoundly revolutionizing effects of the knowledge explosion have been dramatically described by Robert L. Heilbroner in his essays on The Limits of American Capitalism.[5] In his view, the long-term effects of this development will eventually subvert the presently existing societal order as drastically as the new economic incentives of industrial capitalism ultimately destroyed the manorial society of feudalism. One obvious manifestation of this is the tendency of technology to create a society in which an ever wider range of social and economic problems requires a multiplication of administrative controls which in turn interfere with the play of the market forces.

> In part these agencies of control are contained and concealed within the centers of production themselves, where they show up as the rising echelons of corporate administration and supervision that are needed to regulate the underlying traffic of production. In part the controls show up in the familiar bureaus of government that directly oversee the operation of the new technology--the bureaus that cope, with greater or lesser success, with the social repercussions of transportation, nuclear energy, drugs, air pollution, etc.

However, the hegemony of the marketplace--that basic tenet of all contemporary social orders focusing on economics, whether capitalist or communist--is even more fundamentally undermined by a number of other factors. Heilbroner refers to the labor-displacing effects of modern technology, by which he means a gradual shift in the types of work: first, from the agricultural to the industrial, then from the industrial to the services sector, which now increasingly relates to issues of public concern such as urban renewal, education, health and safety standards, recreation facilities (and today we should add: the overriding problems of ecology). In other words, here again there is a strong impetus toward overall organization and planning requiring public action and public funding. And this impetus is likely to become even stronger when a fully automated society will force the question of how the leisured population--now without opportunities for gainful employment in the traditional sense--can be provided with a share in society's output. In addition, there is the impact of technology on the general level of affluence, which may gradually bring about "the end to want." This implication is probably the most portentous of all. It will blunt the drive for profit and free man from the economic necessity to work for a living. Yet, at the same time, it will remove the pivotal assurance of social domestication. Widespread and substantial affluence, once attained, will eliminate the condition of material need as the effective stimulus for the socially obedient behavior it has traditionally been. These latter considerations of Heilbroner's are subject to serious doubt in view of recent developments in the area of ecology. Yet the result remains the same. An impasse will develop for which there seems to be but one possible solution, namely, as Heilbroner puts it: "some authority other than the market must be entrusted with the allocation of men to the essential posts of society. . ."

All this adds up to one unmistakable conclusion. In this new society, the key trend is toward all-encompassing structures of central coordination and control. And as is already strikingly manifest in dominant sectors today, these structures will not only cut across current distinctions--say, between the military and the industrial, the university and the government, or for that matter, between the public and the private--they will also give rise to an interlocking of new elites invested with awesome powers of decision-making.

Running parallel with this trend--but, paradoxically enough, running counter to it as well--there is yet another development, the underlying forces of which have been analyzed in Karl Mannheim's classical study of Man and Society in An Age of Reconstruction.[6] As early as 1935, when the original German edition appeared, Mannheim called attention to two processes which he considered particularly essential to the functioning of modern Western society:

> On the one hand modern industrial society stirs into action those classes which formerly only played a passive part in political life. Let us call this new and far-reaching activity of the masses the fundamental democratization of society. On the other hand, another factor is at work in our society which we will call the process of growing interdependence. This is the ever-increasing degree in which individual activities are being linked up with one another into larger wholes.

Not only did Mannheim regard these processes as basically inherent in "our type of society"; he was also keenly aware that they constitute its principal predicament. To begin with, their effects are cumulative: the greater the number of groups that enter the political arena, the more closely they interact; and the more that occurs, the greater is the need for self-assertion on the part of the ever widening circle of groups whose interests are affected. But the two processes are contradictory as well, the one tending to jeopardize the other. This Mannheim explicated by observing that a modern, fundamentally democratic and thoroughly interdependent society is bound to operate along lines of functional rationality. The organization of the activities of society's members--including their participation in that society--requires a rational system, functionally geared to the attainment of special objectives for each group separately and for all groups together. Such a system, however, is most likely to result in substantial irrationality; that is, the incapacity to act independently and intelligently in a given situation on the basis of one's own insights. Interrelated events are so complex that they baffle any ordinary citizen, leaving him at best in a position of partial participation. They also make him susceptible to the authority of the charismatic "strong man" or to a few "key executives"--the only ones sufficiently capable of possessing an overall view, and/or powerful enough to arrive at independent decisions.

Acting upon this analysis--and especially in view of the devastating implications manifest in the calamities that climaxed in World War II--many of the nations' post-war leaders urgently sought to reconstruct society in order to move it off its collision course and steer it toward "planning for freedom" (Mannheim) or "freedom under planning" (Barbara Wootton). It is the irony of history, however, that the direction of this drive further aggravated the vicious circle in which the modern world was caught. Although there is not the slightest doubt that the new direction produced some firmly secured safeguards for the maximization of democracy, the basic conflict persisted. The tension between the two polarities of interdependence and political action became less easily identifiable--at least for a while--during the reformist activities that preoccupied the 1940's and 1950's. But the pressure kept building up.

All this found clear expression in Western Europe. Here, the terrifying effects of the social, economic and political upheavals of the first half of the century left their deepest scars. And so it was here that efforts aimed at change were most intense and met with widest approval. The generations who had lived through the chaos of the Great Depression and the ensuing totalitarian holocaust, were obsessed with the idea of refashioning the societal order. As a result, there was a definite turn toward the welfare state. Granted, a trend in that direction had already been established well before World War II when governments were forced to intervene in many private sectors of society. Yet compared to that period, developments after the war exhibited an important difference, poignantly expressed by Asa Briggs in reference to Great Britain, the cradle *par excellence* of the true welfare state. Prior to the war, there emerged what Briggs labels the Social Service State--a state employing communal resources in order to alleviate poverty and assist those in distress. But it was not until after 1945 that the full-fledged welfare state appeared on the scene, with a distinctive characteristic:

> the idea of the *optimum* rather than the older idea of the *minimum*. It is concerned not merely with abatement of class

differences or the needs of scheduled groups but with equality of treatment and the aspirations of citizens as voters with equal shares of electoral power.[7]

This new idea contributed decisively to a shift of emphasis in government intervention--a shift from correction to reconstruction. No longer--as in the depression days--did governments take refuge in a haphazard assortment of regulatory measures necessitated by the collapse of the free interplay of forces. Now they embarked on a systematic policy of re-ordering society through a coherent program of short- and long-term national planning. Full employment and the guaranteed right to social security, it was realized, were essential factors for sound and sustained economic growth; and so governments became the backbone of a coordination in which the mechanisms of the private market were subjected to the attainment of publicly set priorities, ensuring both economic and social benefits to the entire population. Broadly-based social-democratic orders then emerged which, by the very nature of their multi-class constituencies, were particularly allergic to the liberalist-bourgeois fallacy that equates freedom with the individual's right to unrestricted command over his private resources. Taught the vastly unequal distribution of such resources by bitter experience, these new orders laid great stress on the structural requirements for ensuring freedom as a collective right--as a <u>de facto</u> reality to all citizens--regardless of social status or economic position. As a result, poverty lost its sting: in fact, it was the common condition of the "austerity economies" prevailing in the immediate post-war period, gradually making way in later years for a condition of steadily rising affluence, administered to the benefit of the national community as a whole through deliberate policies of apportionment.[8]

Due to the realization of this "optimum" concept, many countries of Western Europe reached the stage at which the old egalitarian ideal approximated fulfillment to an unprecedented degree; a degree, that is, well-matched--if not actually superior--to that of American society with its traditional assumption that egalitarianism has always been an integral part of the American way of life. The extent to which the latter assumption rests on foible rather than fact, is soon to be discussed. Here, however, it should be pointed out that now, on both sides of the Atlantic, a socio-political constellation appeared which showed one widely-held conviction: that a truly democratic order had been achieved--thanks either to a strong welfare state redressing the Old World's inequalities of class and status, or to the full maturation of the New World's potentials for universal opportunity and freedom. According to the prevailing view, the basis of this order was a pluralist equilibrium of powers and counterpowers with a broad consensus of opinion about the legitimacy of their claims to inclusion in the decision-making process. It was an order, in other words, which was believed to mark "the end of ideology" and a "de-politicization" of issues, now reduced to predominantly administrative matters that required above all the technical competence and the specialized skills of managing elites.

Whatever the merits of this view, it became quite evident that the two underlying notions of "pluralism" and "consensus" were being increasingly challenged as the 1950's made way for the 1960's. Then--most conspicuously in the United States--these notions demonstrated their shallowness in the face of the suddenly exploding crises within minorities whose plight conflicted sharply with indulgence in liberal rhetoric and middle-class complacency. These were the years of the great démasqué, the shocking exposure of the systematic exclusion of tens of millions of poor and black from the world's wealthiest and most freedom-conscious democracy. The American dream turned out to be a hoax for all those who did not qualify as the comfortably off, securely established, white mainstream society. With the possible exception of the earliest stages of the New Deal, the United States economic and social policies appeared to have been less concerned with fundamental change than with updating and modifying the hallowed principles of nineteenth-century Smithianism.

All this has been abundantly documented in such studies as Michael Harrington's Toward a Democratic Left and Andrew Shonfield's comparative analysis of different styles of Modern Capitalism in the post-war Western world.[9] Thus Shonfield notes that the United States suffered much deeper and more frequent recessions than did Western Europe, while experiencing a significantly lower rate of economic growth, with a bigger proportion of its productive capacity lying idle. He shows this to be due to inherent inadequacies such as insufficient concentration on the objective of full employment, lack of public welfare policies consciously effecting a wide diffusion of rising consumers' incomes, and serious shortcomings in the area of comprehensive long-range planning. These are inherent inadequacies indeed, since they reflect what Shonfield calls the nation's "old problem of the fragmentation of public authority" and its staunch commitment to the--elsewhere outdated--"view . . . of the natural predominance of private enterprise in the economic sphere and of the subordinate role of public initiative in any situation other than a manifest national emergency." Similarly, Harrington's findings leave little doubt as to the paltry nature of such much-acclaimed reform programs as the War on Poverty and the Great Society. Their clever captions à la Madison Avenue notwithstanding, these programs were unmistakably indicative of a "minimum" conception, and furthermore betrayed a basic inability to correct the imbalance between private and public power which lay at the very root of the inequities they allegedly remedied. They supposedly represented welfare state principles. Actually, they mirrored a system which was little more than an ill-disguised device for maximizing government-guaranteed profits for the benefit of private corporations engaged in rendering entrepreneurial services to the publicly-financed relief projects for the structurally dispossessed. The latter were as victimized as ever by the workings of deeply entrenched, institutionalized patterns of exploitation, prejudice, . . . and paternalism.

Indeed, paternalism as well. For a good case can be made for the view that precisely this attribute of the status quo lay at the heart of the issues that spawned the revolt of the 1960's. After all, this revolt was not directed merely at abject forms of economic neglect and racial arrogance. Nor was it a revolt that occurred only in surroundings in which such abuses were prominent. This was already manifest in the United States: the sites of rebellion were not only in the rural areas of utter deprivation, nor in the vast urban ghettos and slums, but also in the nation's poshest college campuses. Of course, all kinds of interrelations existed between these sites and the causes espoused. Yet the feeling of bitter resentment which found expression in poor peoples' campaigns, race riots, anti-war demonstrations, draft-card burnings and university takeovers, did not have as its common bond the issues of poverty and racism--however large such issues loomed, domestically or globally. In the last analysis, this bond was the shared sense of powerlessness, a powerlessness which laid bare the blatant gap between the officially proclaimed myth of "maximum feasible participation" and the exasperating reality of an obvious lack of control over one's own destiny.

The full measure of this gap as the real issue at stake was particularly manifest in western Europe. Here it appeared in its purest form--scarcely clouded by additional tensions resulting from direct involvement in racial strife, economic inequities and acts of war. This is not to say, of course, that western Europe's state of turmoil had nothing to do with the grave problems which rocked the United States--the problems of war and peace, of poverty and race, especially as brought into dramatic focus by the Vietnam conflict. These problems affected the entire world; their implications were felt everywhere. Yet at the same time, it is equally clear that what created havoc in western Europe had deeper roots than mere concern over external matters. In fact, the fierce intensity of the rebellious sentiments was unmistakable evidence of a crisis springing from internal conditions, fundamental to the continent itself.

This crisis was inherent in the very accomplishments of the full-fledged welfare state in its best "optimum" tradition. These accomplishments had evolved from far-reaching reforms so that the class struggles of earlier days had subsided and democracy seemed to have become a solidly-structured, political as well as economic, reality. But the reforms themselves apparently contributed to the emergence of a new rift: a separation between those who benefited from the reforms and those who administered them. The more the process of societal reconstruction was perfected for the sake of democratic inclusiveness, the more it led to a subtle system of checks and balances requiring the coordinative functions and expert services of a new managing elite whose indispensability frustrated rather than facilitated genuine democratic participation. The primary loyalty of this elite was--as it should be!--to the safeguarding and maintenance of an equilibrium between the diversity of interests represented in the national community. To do otherwise, let alone encourage, the advocacy of partisan points of view by particular constituencies might easily upset that equilibrium so carefully nurtured to ensure each constituency's share in the common good. Consequently, a situation emerged which exhibited an increasingly apparent "credibility gap" of Kafkaesque dimensions: the people's right to full participation in the shaping of their corporate destiny turned out to have no real substance unless it was delegated to those in charge of the specialized service institutions and complex coordination procedures essential to the implementation of that right. Or to put it more bluntly: what is such a right actually worth if, in order to reap its benefits, one has to exchange it for virtual dependence upon monopolistic expertise? And to what avail are the reforms which, after having freed the citizen from many forms of paternalisms, now seemed to have come almost full circle by subjecting him to a new paternalism, that of the "servicrats?" These men were in key institutional positions, entrusted with the dispensation of the specialized services vital to the balancing of public and private power.

Autonomy and Interdependence--Twin Principles in Conflict

The "servicrats," together with the technocrats Robert Heilbroner alluded to above, are both the product and the warrant of a society in which the knowledge explosion and the urge for freedom as a collective right created an equalization of liberty on an unprecedented scale. In a word, they constitute the "new class" undergirding the "technopolis" and its scientific and socio-organizational know-how, which constitutes the means for achieving the common good that conditions as well as requires the participation of all. Without this new class the process of fundamental democratization would end in chaos; for without their intervention as society's switchboard operators the inevitable process of interdependence could find no orderly expression. At the same time, and herein lies the paradox: their function as middlemen seriously interferes with the full, unfiltered and unmanipulated, exercise of the rank-and-file's primordial democratic privilege of determining public policy.

This dilemma is not new. It is in fact the basic social question of the modern age, emanating from the two opposing, yet necessarily paired, tendencies inherent in the advance of technology and the espousal of popular sovereignty. For a century and a half these two tendencies have been evident, and definite stages can be distinguished in their continuous striving for prevalence. In the initial stage, autonomy was clearly in the ascendant. This was the period when political and economic liberalism--representing the forces of revolutionary change, successfully challenging autocratic absolutism and restriction-rigged mercantilism--gave rise to a social order which highly valued individual freedom and private initiative, spontaneous self-organization and competitive diversity. Even then, however, interdependence was by no means negligible. From the outset, trends toward national unification and central administration characterized liberalism as well. The forces and values underlying the appeal and thrust of classical liberalism were of a dialectical nature; they entailed further change. Spontaneous self-help and competition, once carried out on a mass basis in conjunction with increasing technological propulsion could not go unchecked--on pain of causing societal self-destruction and oppression. And the same held true for individual freedom and initiative, when these were not coupled with basic provisions to ensure a measure of commonly-shared opportunities for equalizing freedom and initiative. Thus, in this second stage, coordination, rationalization and equality became the basic elements in reordering the society. A case in point, in the western European context, was the eventual emergence of the welfare state, whether of the socio-capitalist or the social-democratic variety, but either way in the "optimum" sense. In the United States, the New Deal and its successors underscored the growing import of federal action over against states' rights and municipal home rule.

More recently, however, it has become fairly obvious that a third stage has been achieved in which the dilemma is aggravated beyond any of its earlier manifestations. The pendulum appears to be swinging back again, but the attraction of each pole is so strong that the result is an inconclusive jerking back and forth or a confused deadlock. Put in graphical form, the following diagram may help to summarize the argument:

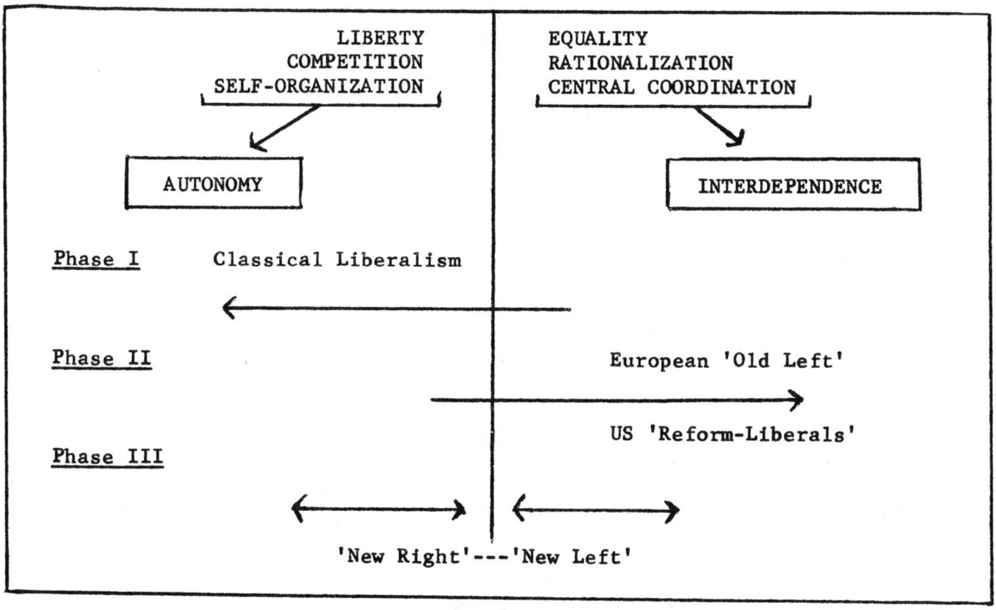

The agonizing question is: how can autonomy and interdependence, which presuppose and hamstring one another, be reconciled? It is like trying to square the circle. The consequent state of confusion is tellingly reflected in the odd amalgam of opposites which seem to contend for mastery among the New Leftists in their open rebellion against the prevailing establishments of the Western world. There can be little doubt that these establishments represent the reigning forces of interdependence against which the rebels of the New Left put up their militant fight for the countercause of autonomy. Yet it is equally apparent that in this fight there has been a curious shifting of positions, blurring dividing-lines of long standing and rendering oblique the once clear-cut labels of conservatism and progressivism. The radical critics--whether they are white SDS'ers, black SNCC'ers, or Red Rudis and Dannies--all express their desire for a new politics. But a closer examination of what this implies reveals a bewildering variety of notions involving entirely divergent facets of the old political spectrum.

To be specific, it is beyond dispute that the New Left stands in the tradition of the Old Left which--as David Caute has characterized the European scene since 1789--is distinctive in "its insistence on popular control and participation."[10] At the same time, however, the New Left appears to hold its major grudge against the Old Left itself, particularly as embodied in United States reform-liberals and western European Social-Democrats. In essence, two reasons, quite paradoxical in nature, account for this. On the one hand, the Old Left is accused of having betrayed the true Left belief in the ongoing class struggle, of having sold out to the lure of affluence present in the neo-capitalist establishment by embracing the theory and practice of pluralism and consensus. Thus, Michael Harrington spoke scornfully of "Adam Smith's Keynesianism" as characteristic of "the economic ideology which the nation received from the New Deal" and has acted upon ever since;[11] while a Provo pamphleteer expressed his disgust with the "material self-interest" underlying present-day society in which the one-time proletariat, joining forces with the bourgeoisie to form "the nauseating middle class," has allowed the old class contrast to be blotted out "through a process of mutual trimming."[12] Or to put it in somewhat less emotionally charged terms, the accusation seems to be well summed up in the following observation of David Caute:

> Once a movement becomes content with adjusting checks and balances, with redistribution, and once it has ceased to attempt to extend the frontiers of popular sovereignty, it has abandoned the dynamic of the Left.

On the other hand, there is the deep distrust of the mushroom growth of "top-down" bureaucracies, a phenomenon for which the Old Left is especially held responsible because of its alleged addiction to planning and centralization. This distrust is by no means unfounded. But it is suggestive of a peculiar inconsistency in the New Left's singling out the Old Left as the particular target. Centralization and planning, after all, are attributes of essential importance to the Left of whatever variety, because of the structural guarantees for implementing its basic tenets of popular control and participation. Accordingly, in chiding the Old Left for sticking to these attributes, the New Left not only appears to argue against its own traditions--which, of course, it has a right to do--but also seems to imply the exact opposite of the earlier accusation: in the one case it infers that the Old Left is not faithful enough to its principles, and the other that it is too faithful.

Similar inconsistencies are evident in the alternatives to which the New Left seeks to give form vis-à-vis the given order of the establishment it so vehemently repudiates. The common denominator of these alternatives is undoubtedly--and in this, once again, they bear witness to their authentic Left pedigree--a zealous craving for a social order with as much justice and individual liberty as possible. These two freedoms inspire visions of a fully participatory, grass-roots democracy--visions in which the mutually restrictive nature of these freedoms is acknowledged in theory, but ignored in practice. One is bound to come to this conclusion in view of the special emphasis characteristic of all the designs of the New Society: the special emphasis on decentralization into a wealth of independent, self-governing constituencies. In the name of the underdog--whether he be the oppressed man of color, the dole recipient, the mass-pressured student, the bureaucracy-dominated rank-and-file citizen--relentless attempts are made at community organization from the bottom up, as the practical means of achieving "black control of the ghetto," "poor people's power," "student syndicalism," "ward republics," or "cameralism from below."[13] However, all these attempts and their motivating blue-prints fall paradoxically short of combating the two dominant forces operating in today's society and against whose implications much of the radical critique is directed.

(1) First, there is the factor of all-inclusiveness, which is an immediate outgrowth of the ideals of liberty and justice for all. In ardently subscribing to these ideals, the New Left aspires to a true pluralism of self-ruling entities. For that very reason it assails the establishment's version of pluralism, which it considers a fake, if not a conspiracy--a conspiracy in which the "ins" play their game of mutual pay-offs that systematically excludes the "outs"; a fake because even the "ins" have in large majority become lame ducks who, while indulging in an unprincipled give-and-take of material rewards, are cajoled into submission to the closed politics of the experts and the executives. It is against this system--run by those who in fact constitute a power elite--that the militant protest movement seeks to organize the disillusioned "outs" and the "ins." The drive is for power for the people so that they can democratically control themselves. But this acute power consciousness which clearly distinguishes the New Left from the naiveté of earlier, doctrinaire anarchism, does not alter the basic anarchist dilemma to which their course so obviously points. That dilemma is not solved by a more sophisticated understanding of power as an absolutely indispensable element in all social relationships rather than an "evil" by definition. The dilemma remains in effect, for its crux lies elsewhere, in the avoidance of the question that arises immediately beyond the horizon of grass-roots politics. Underlying the ability of the people to rule themselves by voluntarily associating in their own, well-understood interests, is the existence of a plurality of communities more or less effectively in charge of their internal affairs. Applying this same principle to the totality of all the communities thus endowed, the next step that inevitably must follow in an all-inclusive society is the demand for an umbrella structure of authority, external to each constituent community, and yet accepted as instrumental to the sharing of liberty by all--which is justice writ large. It is at this point that the New Left appears to be nebulous.

(2) The second factor is increase in scale, which is partly a concomitant of the first, but receives its impetus from the dictates of economic rationalization and technological integration. To advocate decentralization on the basis of communal autonomy, as the New Left does in the face of this factor, involves tremendous odds in more than one sense. Not only does it mean an uphill fight against powerful, material forces driving toward concentration and the rise of corporate centers of control; but it also means a perplexing battle against ideological positions that favor common standards in the service of all citizens. This latter implication especially plays nasty tricks on the New Leftists' aspirations. It tends to push them into a strange alliance with those whose stance is basically reactionary. This sad irony becomes agonizingly manifest in two areas where the need for centralized structures is of vital concern

to the underdogs of today's society. One area is that of metropolitan government. Here, a plea for decentralized home rule is tantamount to adding to what Michael Harrington, describing contemporary America, has aptly termed the "Balkanization" of the urban scene--that is, the chaotic proliferation of petty autarchies bent on perpetuating their privileged status to the exclusion of all the under-privileged.[14] The other area is the classic arena of economic control, in which the cards today are overwhelmingly stacked in favor of superconcentrations of private power, and against attempts at self-help on the part of those without access to comparable resources. It is only through centrally administered and strictly enforced counterchecks in the public interest that a more equitable order can be achieved. And for this reason, the nebulousness of the New Leftists becomes even more baffling since it turns them into unwitting subscribers to that nostalgic fallacy so dear to the conservatives of old and new vintage alike--namely, that one needs only to trust the Smithian *deus ex machina* of the Invisible Hand to ensure harmony between the competing interests of the lions and the lambs.

To summarize, we must conclude that the New Left zeal for a society in which there is both true liberty and true equality still lacks an approach that steers clear of old pitfalls. In fact, its course appears to be slanted in a way detrimental to effective equalization of power bases, whose uneven distribution mars all rhetoric--including that of the New Left--about participatory democracy. Having said this, however, another conclusion must be drawn as well. Whatever its theoretical inadequacies, the rebellious outcry against the existing order is primarily inspired by the pragmatic necessity of breaking the deadlock between autonomy and interdependence. A vast majority of the citizenry seems resigned to this condition, complacent in a present that for many has erased the deprivations of the past; but a deadlock still exists, and it carries with it injustices of its own. These augment the injustices suffered by the many for whom neither past nor present have brought a substantial change. It was with keen awareness of this that, in the 1960's, the revolutionary impulse of the deprived made common cause with the protest against the smug middle class and their preoccupation with material security. This coalescence produced a movement that raised anew the banner of man's quest, a movement willing to act as the vanguard of challenge.

NOTES AND REFERENCES

Chapter III

1. The Triple Revolution, by The Ad Hoc Committee on The Triple Revolution (Santa Barbara, Calif., 1964).

2. "Technopolis," Harvey Cox, The Secular City (New York: The MacMillan Company, 1965), pp. 5 f. Techno-polis is an apt term indeed, combining in one word the two basic elements shaping contemporary society: technology, affecting all aspects of life, and "polis," i.e. the community of all citizens who cannot afford the luxury of staying out of the decision-making process (= politics).

3. An illustration of the relationship between big power responsibilities and the ability to focus on domestic concerns, may be found in the following comparative data: in 1968, according to the State of the Union report, the United States spent 53 per cent of its national budget on "defense" over against 11 per cent on "social and economic progress" (including education); for the Netherlands, in 1960, the comparable figures were 26.7 and 33.2 per cent respectively--that is, half as much and three times more! 1960 budget figures, the Netherlands. P. E. Kraemer, The Societal State (Meppel/Holland: J. A. Boom & Zoon, 1966), p. 48.

4. "Provos," Duco van Weerlee, Wat de Provo's Willen (Amsterdam: De Bezige Bij, 1966), p. 19. For a translation of this brochure, Rebels With A Cause, UTC Pamphlet No. 1 (Chicago: The Urban Training Center, 1967), pp. 15-39.

5. Robert L. Heilbroner, The Limits of American Capitalism (New York: Harper & Row, 1966), esp. pp. 118 f.

6. Karl Mannheim, Man and Society in An Age of Reconstruction (London: Routledge & Kegan Paul, 1948), pp. 44 f., 52 f.

7. Asa Briggs, "The Welfare State in Historical Perspective," in Archives Européennes de Sociologie, 1961, p. 228 (underlining is mine, P.E.K.).

8. "Correction to reconstruction," Kraemer, Societal State, pp. 51 f.

9. Andrew Shonfield, Modern Capitalism (New York/London: Oxford University Press, 1965), chs. I (pp. 15-16), IV, XIII (p. 298), XIV (p. 336); Michael Harrington, Toward a Democratic Left (New York: The MacMillan Company, 1968), chs. II-IV.

10. David Caute, The Left in Europe since 1789 (New York/Toronto: World University Library, McGraw-Hill Book Company, 1966), pp. 31, 43, 44. In quoting Caute, it should be made clear that we do not follow here his distinction between the Old and New Left which he designates as the "political" (Jacobin) and "economic" (Marxist, both orthodox and revisionist) Lefts, respectively. Instead, we take these two together and oppose them—in accordance with current, popular terminology--as Old Left to the recently emerged, New Left protest.

11. Harrington, Toward a Democratic Left, p. 36.

12. Provo pamphleteer. Van Weerlee, Rebels With a Cause, p. 28.

13. Cameralism-from-below. A concept developed by Stoughton Lynd, in a seminar at The Urban Training Center, Chicago, January, 1968.

14. "Balkanization," Harrington, Toward a Democratic Left, pp. 132, 152; also his "Taking the Great Society Seriously," Harper's, December, 1966, p. 47.

PART TWO:

EMANCIPATION MOVEMENTS --

AN ANATOMICAL INTERLUDE

> Anybody who asks where it is going should look first at where it comes from, and how, hitherto, it has fared.
>
> Denis de Rougemont[1]

CHAPTER IV

EMANCIPATION FOR WHAT?

A TYPOLOGY AND TENTATIVE CLASSIFICATION

While the movement of the 1960's possessed particular American features, it must, at the same time, be viewed in a much wider perspective. Thus far, only one dimension of this perspective has been explored--the dimension of space. This has led to the conclusion that the movement-for-change on the American scene is part of a dual upsurge clearly manifest on many other scenes today. The one is the worldwide emergence of the colored nations inspired by the "globalization" of the material and ideological revolution of rising expectations; the other is the equally universal tide of revolutionary sentiments among a new generation whose members both challenge and are provoked by the ideals and achievements of a democratic-technological order which is being put to the test of a truly "inclusive pluralism."

There is a time factor as well. This will be examined here in a special way. Our intention is not so much to look back at the movement and its antecedents in United States history, but rather to probe the developments of other movements of a kindred nature, though occurring under different circumstances and in different historical settings. In other words, we shall attempt to probe the tradition in which the American movement stands and to gain some insights from the resulting, comparative framework--the framework of developments in social change which can be characterized as "emancipation movements."

Emancipation Movements As Programmatic Movements

Throughout history, social movements have risen in opposition to whatever was keeping particular groups in bondage. In a sense, all such movements aimed at emancipation--that is, liberation from some sort of coercive authority imposed from outside and sanctioned by the established power relationships. Sometimes these relationships rested purely on the exercise of physical force; more often, however, they had become embedded in a hierarchy of values and a corresponding pattern of institutional arrangements that had gained predominance under a certain set of conditions prevalent over a long period of time. Resistance emerged for various reasons. Segments of the population may have risen in blind anger and utter despair because of unendurable hardship; they may have rebelled against and fought for the overthrow of a system that subjected them to domestic subservience or foreign domination; or they may have awakened to visions of a future society in which no moral justification for special privileges could exist. Cases in point range from the slave revolts in ancient Rome or nineteenth century America, to peasant jacqueries, religious reformations, and nationalist risorgimentos in the Old World, the New World, or the Third World; from agitations by abolitionists, suffragettes, and ethnic and cultural minorities to revolutions of the bourgeois "third estate," the proletarian "fourth estate," the colored "underclasses," the "underdeveloped nations," or the alienated new generation styling themselves "the 'de-class' of the provotariat."[2]

In this general sense, movements rejecting the status quo have been in evidence ever since recorded history. More specifically, however, the term "emancipation"--especially as it is understood in modern social thought--does not apply to all these movements.[3] Emancipation movements are a distinct phenomenon of the new era--uniquely new, as many claim--that emerged from the dynamics of the French and Industrial Revolutions. What characterizes these movements is not a wild outburst of enraged despair--something that we find throughout the ages. On the contrary, the essential feature of emancipation movements is an element of hopeful anticipation of an order in which no man can be prevented from coming into his own. Thus understood, such movements are programmatic; they are irrepressible uprisings of the deprived, dreaming dreams that no longer need to go unfulfilled but can be realized through the full utilization of the rich resources so demonstrably available.

Even so, emancipation movements of this particular type--hereafter we shall refer to them exclusively--cannot be lumped together indiscriminately. Although essentially identical, especially when contrasted with other social movements caused by elemental fury, they still exhibit marked differences which we will divide into two major categories.

Theoretically, the question raised by the present chapter is: emancipation for what? Perhaps this seems a rather rhetorical question. Emancipation movements are movements for change, for fundamental change. They do not merely lash out against the historical status quo, but also envision and strive toward a new order of relationships that substitutes equality for subjugation. They imply vast shifts in deeply rooted attitudes and patterns of behavior, both on the part of the dominating forces and those struggling to overcome the effects of long-standing degradation; and so they also imply equally vast shifts in values and institutions. However, there are different degrees of change involved in these shifts--depending upon the existing relationships within a particular society, or between various societies for that matter. For instance, the dominant element may be the exponent of a way of life that basically holds sway over all the people but which, in actual practice, is beyond the reach of certain groups. Such groups--for whatever reason--fail to meet the criteria of inclusion laid down and institutionally safeguarded by the established wielders of power. Or the dominant element may represent a completely closed system, acknowledging no legitimacy other than that dictated by its own self-interest. This creates a condition of total alienation on the part of any aspirant to the contrary. In both cases, the emancipation process entails reorientation, revaluation, and restructuring--although the degree varies widely as does the ultimate perspective which motivates the process, lends force to and directs it. The kind of order an emancipation movement seeks to achieve--in which authority is no longer experienced as external coercion but derives from internal acceptance through effective autonomy--can be correlated with the need of the existing order to be changed. The future envisioned projects an inverse image of today's reality. The greater the obstacles to be removed, in fact or in the opinion of those excluded, the more likely it is that the final goal will be understood in terms of revolution rather than reform.

On the basis, then, of such considerations, two types of movements suggest themselves, one tending toward a reordering of an assimilatory nature, the other toward a radical reconstruction, fully transformative in character:

TYPE I	TYPE II
ASSIMILATORY	TRANSFORMATIVE
Degree of change	Degree of change
↕ relatively limited, opening and widening the inclusiveness of given system into a reformed whole	total rupture with given system, building a completely new, transformed order ↕
Ultimate perspective	Ultimate perspective

In Type I movements, the degree of change is relatively limited, although by no means insignificant, for it eventually requires the existing order to be broken open and reconstituted into a new whole. The result will be <u>assimilation</u>, that is the integration of the emancipatory element (Ee) into the larger system of the widened, mainstream dominant (Md). This larger system may not be completely unlike its earlier form, yet it operates according to a different formula of inclusiveness, a formula now equally co-determined by the new element, and thus considerably affecting those who formerly were in sole control.

In Type II movements, on the other hand, far more drastic changes are implied--as the following pair of diagrams attempts to show:

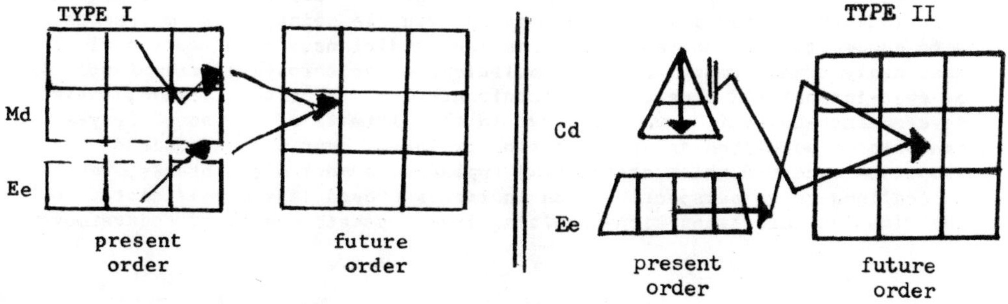

The second case requires a total transformation, the emergence of a completely new order out of the radically reshuffled relationships between the previously separate and essentially dissimilar parts, namely the closed dominant (Cd) and the subjected, emancipatory element (Ee). The existing system must be eradicated because it is fundamentally exclusive and oppressive. There is no possibility of appeal to common values, let alone common enjoyment of such values; equality of terms can be achieved only on the basis of an entirely new set of values which will explode the old order, its underlying principles, and supporting institutions.

Emancipation Movements Sorted

In visualizing, in the above schemes, the two opposite types of emancipation movements, it becomes clear that theoretical notions, rather than empirical realities, prevail. In other words, the typology is an ideal-typical one, a construct of the mind which magnifies to the extreme what are actually relative positions. It is an analytical tool applicable to a variety of emancipation movements as they have appeared at different times and places. This method is not pursued for its own sake, but in order to provide a classificatory framework of historical movements, within which a more specific answer can then be sought to the question: how does the United States movement compare to these other movements, and what, essentially, do they involve?

In developing this framework, the following three points should be kept in mind:

(1) Attention cannot be focused exclusively on the extremes, the poles of the construct; it is necessary to focus on the whole continuum. The historical data pertains to living organisms subject to shifts in their ultimate goals as well as in their internal dynamics, in relation to changes occurring in external conditions, or in their perception of them. Consequently, it is sometimes hard to make clear-cut distinctions as to type--which is a point worth noting as having particular bearing upon this study's principal concern: the understanding of the United States movement and "where it is at" today;

(2) Generally speaking, the movements to be analyzed achieved liberation and consequent societal change without actual revolution, in the sense of an abrupt and drastic (and often violent) reversal of power relationships. Viewed from a post factum vantage point, these movements were successful in substantially altering conditions, if not more or less thoroughly transforming the socio-political order through a gradual process of ever-intensified pressures and confrontations. For that reason, their development--however "revolutionary" in the ultimate effect on society--can best be described as an "evolutionary" one. Even though sudden eruptions occurred which at the time appeared to be radical breaks, yet in the long-range perspective such incidents proved less significant than the slow but sure transition resulting from repeated moves and countermoves;

(3) In selecting the empirical movements to be classified tentatively, it seems advisable to select them from diverse cultural settings. The reason for this is that each "culture" is likely to have its particular experience with such movements, and these experiences tend to determine the general notion about what appears to be typical. A cross-cultural approach, therefore, can broaden the base of generalizations, or at least help to determine whether different cultural settings reveal different, similar, or additional ideas. The validity of this procedure is suggested by the cross-cultural dimensions that are inherent in the United States movement as defined in the preceding chapters. In its present form, this movement is the product of forces that go beyond the American dream, or even the Western quest, but are inspired by the awakening of those in conflict with the presumption of western or white supremacy. As a result, any attempt to put a movement of this nature into a broader, more comparative perspective, requires that the constituent items be selected accordingly. They should be selected from at least the three distinct cultural milieus from which this movement-for-change receives its basic impetus--the United States itself, Europe as the cradle of ideologies, old and new, and the emergent Third World. To do otherwise would be a grave error, not only from a scholarly point of view, but also because any Westerner takes a risk when he unconsciously, if not subconsciously, tries to shape reality according to his own Occident-centered image, however diversified it may be.

Focusing then on the United States, various movements suggest themselves for consideration. First, there is the abolitionist movement with which "emancipation" is perhaps most closely identified historically. Yet it is doubtful whether an examination of this movement can add much to the insights specifically sought here. Abolitionism definitely served the emancipatory cause of a victimized people; but it contributed more toward easing the pangs of conscience suffered by the enlightened elite than to heralding a new dawn of self-determination for the destitute minority. The Declaration of Emancipation of 1863, which set all slaves free, did mark the beginning, rather than the end, of the struggle for liberation-on-their-own-terms as waged by those most directly involved. For this reason, all that occurred before 1863 lacks the basic characteristic of emancipation movements under consideration here--movements issuing from the disenfranchised masses themselves, aware of the incompatibility of their condition with the new order they anticipate. This characteristic, however, is present in several other movements on American soil, most conspicuously in the sequence of immigrant groups of diverse ethnic stock whose fight for acceptance in the mainstream of society is part of the American experience. These groups, therefore, explicitly qualify for this inquiry's analytical purpose.

The particular vicissitudes experienced by these ethnic immigrants--of Caucasian extraction--leave little doubt as to which of the two types of emancipation movements they belong.[4] They arrived in wave upon wave throughout the nineteenth and early twentieth century; first the uprooted from Germany and Scandinavia, then those from Ireland, followed by hundreds of thousands from Italy, the Balkan countries, Poland and Russia. All encountered the same problem: discrimination by those who, having come earlier, considered themselves the true representatives of "native" America and were jealous of preserving their newly-established way of life. In varying degrees, the successive groups of newcomers suffered the stigma of inferiority due to their differences in culture, religion, and language, and their lowly socio-economic status; but this inferiority could be overcome as they gradually achieved the marks of respectability that ensured full membership in the society which they had chosen as their new haven. They entered as minorities, struggled through the tensions caused by their desire to retain their distinctive heritage and the urge to overcome the handicaps imposed by this distinctiveness, and finally became a part of the majority. In other words, the emancipation process involved was essentially an assimilatory one; and so the location on the typological continuum can be approximated as follows:

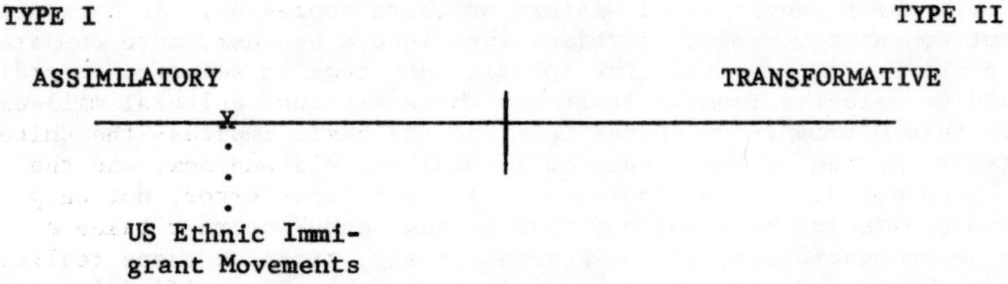

The foreign immigrants ultimately became integrated into the dominant mainstream which, although enlarged and enriched in the process, remained fundamentally the same determinant, requiring an adjustment to its conception of "nativeness." The basic quarrel, in short, was not necessarily with the given order, but with the denial of acceptance by it. This proved particularly hard to bear in a society dedicated to the equality of all men. But tension disappeared as soon as the excluded achieved acceptance.

A similar conclusion applies to the _labor unions_ in the United States. To a certain extent, this resulted from the instrumental role of labor organizations in the immigrants' fight for improved economic and social status. In fact, these organizations often were important and effective weapons in the intrigue which the newcomers, who had nothing to offer but their hands, had to employ in order to gain entry into the dominant majority. But even if we consider the labor unions solely as a movement _per se_, the same conclusion is generally valid. In making this statement we take note of the existence of two distinctly identifiable branches which reflect basic trends which (as shall be discussed later) also affect the labor movement elsewhere. In the United States, they can roughly be equated with the two major union federations, the American Federation of Labor (AFL) and the Congress of Industrial Organization (CIO). The late appearance of the latter in 1935--seceding from the former which dates back to 1886--indicates the extent to which the more conservatively-oriented, and less ideology-conscious, associations of trades and craftsmen dominated the development of American unionism.[5] This domination experienced a brief intermezzo in the 1930's when, during a period of grave economic crisis, the CIO united new organizations of workers in mass-production industries. This drive "represented the most radical point yet reached by labor in the United States," as a long-time CIO-activist, James Boggs, puts it.[6] The drive did not last, however. "The end of the CIO," according to this same observer, came (by means of a merger with the AFL in the early 1950's) when it failed to live up to the principle "that all organizations that spring up in a capitalist society and do not take absolute power, but rather fight only on one tangential or essential aspect of that society, are eventually incorporated into capitalist society."[7] This criticism, which may mirror the bitterness of disillusionment, still finds support in the arguments propounded by others, less directly involved in militant unionism, who view America's recent social history from a broader perspective. The arguments of men like Louis Hartz or Andrew Shonfield, for example, make clear that whatever elements of radical reform the New Deal era may have attempted to effect, little was accomplished beyond "deflated Whiggery" and a pragmatic course of technical adjustments that fell far short of fundamental reconstruction along non- or anti-capitalist lines.[8] There is therefore persuasive evidence of the abortive nature of the new unions' societal critique, due to their piecemeal rather than frontal assault. In the long run, they had little choice but to return to the fold of the old unions that meanwhile had become powerful partners of the former sole determinants of established order. And so in the final analysis, it seems fair to conclude that the United States labor movement has generally tended toward assimilation, in spite of a brief eruption of opposite tendencies. Put in schematic form, the following classification results:

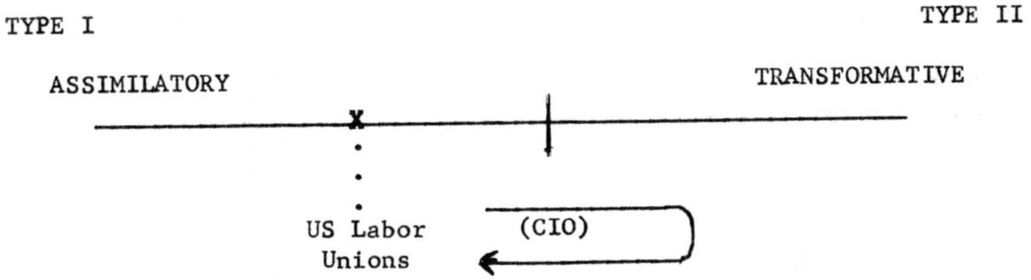

Shifting focus and looking across the Atlantic, the <u>European labor movement</u> as a whole presents a quite different picture. Here too uniformity does not exist; in fact, its absence is even more conspicuous because of national idiosyncracies and, above all, a wealth of bi-, sub-, and cross-furcations issuing from the basic trends alluded to before. Europe has witnessed a proliferation of forms. At least three principal orientations can be distinguished: liberal (or rather liberalist), socialist, and confessional (Roman Catholic/Protestant), each one of which again produced all sorts of internal divisions, in addition to the products of crossbreeding.[9] Yet it is beyond question that, in contrast to the United States, Europe's labor movement has been dominated throughout by radically reformist or even revolutionary motivated unions. This has been the case almost from the very beginning of the formation of workers' associations and has determined the standard with which subsequent groups were compelled to comply.

In the earliest stages, the skilled craft unions could have had real significance by raising the issue of workmen's rights, but their collaboration with, and consequent dependence on, the self-styled <u>bourgeois</u>

illuminés in politics and management soon shunted them on to a siding. They simply were no match for the ideologues of class conflict, who awakened the toiling masses to the need to overthrow existing society's "base-" and "superstructures." By the same token, the confessionally-inspired organizations which emerged at later stages, found themselves involved in a continuous battle combining an effort to hold their own against doctrine of materialist humanism with a genuine attempt to establish a more just social order. But even so--whatever the peculiar motivations and viewpoints--the basic drive was toward thorough reconstruction, through both economic and closely allied political movements propelled by ideological blue-prints. These blue-prints ranged from Owenite utopias of sorts to Rerum Novarum programs-of-solidarism to Marxist designs-of-scientific-prophecy spelling the doom of oppressive capitalism and heralding the classless society. Granted, this richly diversified movement went through many phases, frequently suffered bitter failures, lost momentum, regained it, and changed in the process; but in its totality, it brought about a substantial reordering, injecting new values and shaping new institutions.[10] In short, as an emancipatory movement it not only affected the status and position of the working classes seeking to cast off the bonds of deprivation, but it also proved a significant force in transforming the entire society. Visually expressed again, the diagram can be presented as follows:

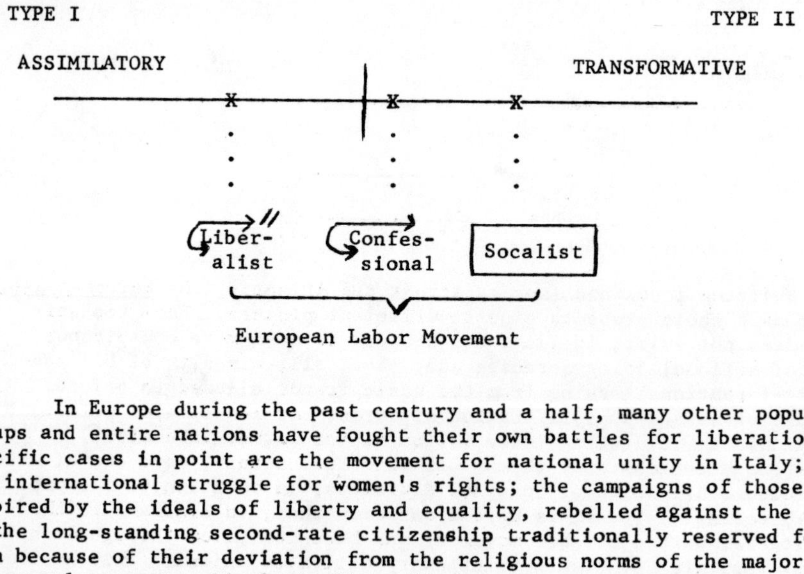

In Europe during the past century and a half, many other population groups and entire nations have fought their own battles for liberation. Specific cases in point are the movement for national unity in Italy; the international struggle for women's rights; the campaigns of those who, inspired by the ideals of liberty and equality, rebelled against the onus of the long-standing second-rate citizenship traditionally reserved for them because of their deviation from the religious norms of the majority. In several respects--ideologically and otherwise--these movements appeared in almost as great a variety of forms as the workers' unions and allied organizations; often this was hardly coincidental but demonstrated the relationship between elements springing from the same basic sources and with closely parallel goals. Yet, these movements have peculiar characteristics of their own and therefore require consideration. This will be done by singling out a particular movement, the selection of which does not so much serve pars pro toto purposes, but rather is based on special qualities that seem relevant to the main subject matter of this study. We have selected the Roman Catholics in the Netherlands because it is a movement that reveals dimensions remarkably similar to certain salient features of the contemporary American movement, especially in relation to black power and black identity.

Since the seventeenth century when the Netherlands emerged as a national entity from the prolonged struggle against Spain--then the center of power of the crumbling Holy Roman Empire and the Habsburg dynasty--this Protestant nation had stigmatized the country's Roman Catholic population as a tolerated but discriminated against minority. The situation was by no means rectified by the new constitutions of 1795 and 1848, which laid the cornerstones of full political democracy. On the contrary, the official proclamation of constitutionally guaranteed freedoms regardless of creed and hereditary status only accentuated the degree of inferiority from which Roman Catholic citizens suffered. Subjected to century-old practices of exclusion that denied them access to virtually all opportunities and resources for self-development--a circumstance aggravated by their geographic concentration in a part of the country farthest removed from the central loci of political power, economic activity, and cultural growth--these people faced a condition of almost total disparagement. Not only were they victims of the traditional ostracism practiced by their Protestant compatriots, but they themselves had grown accustomed to acquiescence in their lowly position, so eroding was their experience. A crucial element, therefore, in their emancipation, was the rebirth of self-respect, the rediscovery of their distinct identity, and the forging of a proud unity rooted in the unique qualities of their common cultural heritage. This was inspired by a renewed belief in the values of that heritage, as demonstrated in the past and inspiring their future. It is this which, more than anything else, became the rallying force. It led to a sustained effort to weld all segments of the community into a phalanx of agents and institutions owing their allegiance to that which set them apart: their Catholic faith. This unmistakable trend toward separatism--greatly enhanced by demographic differentials which made it likely that some day numerical superiority would be theirs--was a prerequisite for proving one's worth. It became the spearhead of a drive to dethrone Protestantism. For a considerable time, this movement seemed to be aiming at a takeover; the Protestant nation would be remade into a Roman Catholic one. Subsequent developments, however, resulted in a gradual lessening of the movement's confessional emphasis. Confronted with a variety of ideologies and their appeal to the masses--whose vital interests were less affected by historical dichotomies, like creeds, than by the issues of societal redistribution emerging from a new, revolutionary age--the emphasis became more diffuse. Some elements tended to opt for a cultural pluralism, others expressed explicit concern for political and socio-economic reorganization. So, in the long run, the Roman Catholic emancipation movement struck a balance between assimilation into a more truly pluralist Dutch society and the transformation of that society into an order of greater social justice:

TYPE I — ASSIMILATORY | TYPE II — TRANSFORMATIVE

Roman Catholic Movement
in the Netherlands

Finally, attention should be paid to emancipation movements which--however much they may have been kindled by the infusion of Western values and dynamics--found their deepest inspiration in the resurgence of old, authentic cultures. These movements took the shape of struggles for national liberation, but there was much more at stake than political independence or the destruction of foreign schemes for economic exploitation. These movements sought the total reversal of an epoch and challenged the arrogant cultural colonialism which forced its parochialism on other civilizations. This is obvious from the electrifying shock that reverberated throughout the entire world when Japan, a nation never subjected to the humiliation of losing its independence, defeated the Russian fleet and armies in 1905. It was this event which, especially in Asia, set off a reaction that would eventually prove uncontainable, bringing about a global confrontation of richly diversified heritages. For illustrative purposes, a brief survey of some specific developments may suffice.

In the Indonesian nationalist movement--as in virtually all the anti-colonialist movements of Asia and the Middle East--three stages can be distinguished, each with its own particular emphasis. The earliest stage coincided with the start of this century when Japan accomplished its historic feat. China witnessed the Boxer rebellion, and the names of Sun Yat-sen and Gandhi became associated with the revolutionary stirrings of Asia's oldest civilizations. The emphasis was on cultural revival. This found unmistakable expression in the first organized forms of Indonesia's budding attempt at self-assertion--the Society "Budi Utomo," founded in 1908 by Javanese intellectuals and aristocrats, plus the "Sarekat Islam" and "Muhammadyah" movements.[11] These date from 1911-12 and appealed to the larger, overwhelmingly Mohammedan masses. Characteristic of all three pioneer organizations was their great concern about opportunities for indigenous schooling and reflection. This concern was motivated by the cultural and especially the religious reform tendencies that had begun to appear throughout the entire world east of the Mediterranean. The aggressive inroads of the Christian West and all it implied, spiritually and materially, at long last precipitated the reawakening of the peoples of the Orient. Both elitist and mass-based initiatives responded to the challenge of modernization by reasserting as well as reinterpreting the values of their millennia-old civilizations. This quest for revitalization of rich and ancient traditions was most effectively pursued by seizing upon the very instruments by which the colonialist powers had introduced the subjected nations to the allegedly superior ways of the West--the schools and institutions responsible for the transference of cultural treasures. This particular impetus, which through the years would remain active as a forceful undercurrent, soon lost its initial non-political character and broadened into a wider movement. In the case of the "Sarekat Islam," this was immediately evident: the search for intellectual and spiritual identity was directly coupled with promotion of mutual economic support and gave rise to a multitude of cooperative societies. What began as a religious social movement inevitably widened its scope and gradually became a socio-political movement.

In the second stage, begun during the unsettling period following World War I, strong influences began to raise the fundamental issue of national self-determination. At the time, however, instead of focusing on the immediate achievement of full national independence, most of the movement's vitality was absorbed in an intensive debate about the ultimate social perspective within which this objective should be pursued. Of course, the two could not be separated. Consequently, this period did not lack militant spokesmen who advocated the colonial regime's overthrow as the prerequisite for the building of a new society based on a merger of indigenous culture and both ideological and material inputs derived from the Western world-in-transition. Yet, though discussion raged about the feasibility of implanting socialist reconstruction schemes on Asian soil, existing power conditions prompted the majority to follow a more expedient course--acquisition of self-rule concessions through collaboration with the enlightened elements among the foreign administrators. This so-called cooperative approach also extended into the third stage which evolved while World War II was dealing irreparable blows to Europe's colonial empires. But gradually the emphasis shifted toward an all-out effort to throw off the foreign yoke and gain control of one's national destiny, politically, economically, and culturally. The final goal from which there was to be no deviation became absolute national sovereignty, achieved by any means, military or diplomatic; complete eradication of colonialist exploitation; and dedication to the reordering of both national and international society on Socialist-inspired principles. Thus as an emancipation movement, the Indonesian nationalist movement, went through several different phases, yet showed great consistency in its ultimate goal of self-assertion, necessarily requiring almost total transformation:

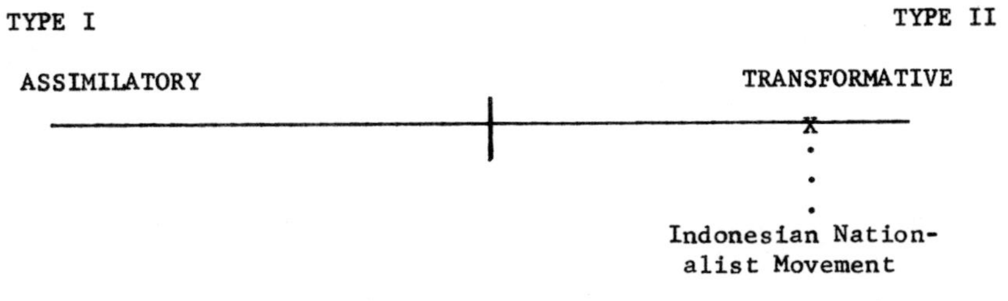

Of all five movements discussed, the Indonesian nationalist movement clearly comes closest to representing a radical rupture with the past and the building of a new, fully reconstructed order. To a degree this reflects this movement's rather exceptional position with respect to typology. This is the only movement with a final goal which was not and could not be achieved without an actual revolutionary break. National independence by definition implied an ouster of the foreign regime. Viewed from another angle, however, Indonesia's nationalist cause was only part of a much wider emancipation movement encompassing all the ex-colonized peoples of the Third World. Not only did they attempt to gain political sovereignty as individual nations but also to challenge the economic and cultural imperialism of the non-colored superpowers, whether American or European, capitalist or Soviet-Communist. In this context then, there can be little doubt that a substantial transformation has occurred over the last few decades, a transformation resulting not from the overthrow of the ex-colonial powers, but involving a complete change in the relationship between these powers and the new nations, now bound together in inescapable worldwide interdependence.

NOTES AND REFERENCES

Chapter IV

1. Denis de Rougemont, Man's Western Quest (New York: Harper & Brothers, 1956, 1957), p. 196.

2. This is the way, for instance, in which a Dutch Provo conceived of the movement he participated in. He was engaged in a rousing provocation of "the disinterested sleeping dummies" among whom "the former class contrast between bourgeoisie and proletariat doesn't exist any more" and "the progressive revolutionary dash has petered out." Van Weerlee, Rebels With A Cause, pp. 27-28.

A similar self-conception seemed apparent in the U.S. Yippies, as represented by such a spokesman as Abbie Hoffman and his Revolution for the Hell of It (New York: The Dial Press, 1968).

3. Emancipation. A. Dorner, "Emancipation," Encyclopaedia of Religion and Ethics, ed. by James Hastings (Edinburgh/New York: T. & T. Clark/Charles Scribner's Sons, 1908-1926), Vol. V; J. A. A. van Doorn & C. J. Lammers, Moderne Sociologie (Utrecht/Antwerpen: Aula-Boeken, 1959), pp. 293 f.

4. Orientals (principally Chinese and Japanese) and Latin-Americans (Mexicans and Puerto-Ricans) constitute a different case; the former, as Joseph Huthmacher makes very clear, were subject to what he characterizes as "immigration exclusion," the latter to "immigration restriction." J. Joseph Huthmacher, A Nation of Newcomers (New York: Dell Publishing Company, 1967), chs. IV, V.

5. The CIO was actually formed in 1938, out of the Committee of Industrial Organization which seceded in 1935.

6. James Boggs, The American Revolution. Pages from a Negro Worker's Notebook (New York: Monthly Review Press, 1963), pp. 16-32.

7. In contrast to the U.S. radical unions which fought "only on one . . . aspect" of the society, the European labor movement fought on various aspects--economic, political, cultural. This is particularly evident in the Socialist labor movement, which not only established a close alliance of economic unions and political parties, but also was committed to the development of a new "proletarian" culture and life style, especially by means of (anti-clerical) free-thinkers' societies, temperance leagues and, most important, (non-bourgeois) youth organizations.

8. Louis Hartz, The Liberal Tradition in America (New York: Harcourt, Brace & World, 1955), esp. chs. IX, X; Shonfield, Modern Capitalism, pp. 309 f.

9. The term "liberalist" is certainly preferable here, as it connotes the specifically historic position of economic and political liberalism which reigned supreme in nineteenth century, Western societies; in contrast to the much more general term "liberal" which conveys particularly as used in the United States, an attitude of reform-mindedness.

10. Here again attention must be called to the contrast between the American and European labor movements, a contrast in the number of aspects of the society they assailed (see footnote 7).

11. "Budi Utomo" etc., Bernard H. M. Vlekke, Nusantara (Cambridge, Mass.: Harvard University Press, 1954), pp. 335 f.

CHAPTER V

AN EMANCIPATION MOVEMENT'S LIFE-CYCLE: A THREE-DIMENSIONAL MODEL

Before attempting to locate the United States movement on the typological continuum as developed and applied in the previous chapter, a further examination of the emancipation movement as evolving organism is in order. As earlier indicated, any classification in terms of two polar types can only be tentative. The reasons are plain: all emancipation movements show a mixture of both assimilatory and transformative tendencies, allowing at best rough approximations of where a particular movement actually fits into the theoretical structure; moreover, each single movement goes through a sequence of developmental stages that may or may not vary in typological nature. This observation has already been made in prior discussions and diagrams. But so far the major emphasis has been on a general assessment of the respective movements as a whole, seen as static entities.

To give due consideration to both the process of internal and of external dynamics requires additional analysis. This analysis will try to isolate certain patterns in the development of an emancipation movement from early emergence to final achievement. Such patterns may be assumed to exist in any movement which necessarily consists of actors and actions, motivations and motifs, resulting in a flow of events and ensuing redirections. The particular forms in which this occurs shall now be investigated by means of a composite case study of several emancipation movements as they have unfolded historically. The selection of such movements is guided by the following considerations: (1) the establishment of a general life-cycle model based on empirical data pertaining to movements that (2) have been classified under various headings in the assimilation-transformation typology; and (3) have appeared within a number of cultural settings, while (4) exhibiting elements that seem significantly relevant to the many-faceted characteristics of the United States movement. So, four movements present themselves as especially appropriate for examination: American ethnic immigrant groups, Europe's working-classes, Holland's Roman Catholics, and the ex-colonial world's nationalists, as exemplified by Indonesia.

The Emancipation Movement in Relation to its Own Components

Emancipation movements generally consist of a variety of elements which represent different points of view or interests, and may at different times have a quite different impact on the movement and its course. This circumstance makes it advisable to focus, first of all, on a movement's internal dynamics.

It can be established that all of the movements under consideration here began to emerge under conditions that students of the social and economic history of nineteenth-century Europe have characterized as those of the so-called Situation Class.[1] The victims of a given societal constellation submit in mute resignation to their fate, enduring it apathetically as an unalterable fact of life. It is against this situation that the earliest instigators of the movement had to wage their first battles. The people had to be aroused to an awareness of their condition; they had to be shaken free from their meek acceptance of a situation that violated their human dignity. The idea of human dignity may not have been new in itself, but it could only become a powerful inspirational appeal that moved masses and touched consciences within an environment in which the notions of freedom and equality had become universal motifs. This was evident in all four movements. The ethnic immigrants in the United States found themselves condemned to a life hardly--if at all--different from that of their forebears in the Old World. And yet they had arrived on the shores of a land promising liberty and plenty. The European working-classes and the Dutch Roman Catholics knew only traditional subjection as virtual outcasts. Yet they lived in a society that sowed the seeds of man's natural rights to full citizenship and social and economic justice. The colonized people had been degraded through centuries of foreign exploitation and emasculation; still they felt the impact of a global civilization founded upon the principles of national self-determination and the promise of spiritual and material self-expression. In short, past experience had taught all these groups to acquiesce in their suffering. Yet their milieu held out hope for a new future that could be seized through concerted efforts.

It is to these possibilities that the few sought to awaken the many, by appealing to the basic values of common identity--values neglected and despised by the dominant culture, but now proudly reinterpreted as the unifying source of the individual's intrinsic and collective worth. The emphasis was on the affirmation of whatever was characteristic of the group's heritage or condition--nationality or language, religion or total cultural orientation, or even a proletarian existence. All this kindled the flames of solidarity and illuminated the vision of a new humanity freed from debasing and corrupting bondage. This characteristic was to be the origin of the self-respect that was indispensable in order to be respected in a society which loftily proclaimed the equality of all human beings while disdainfully denying it to those who do not uncompromisingly force recognition of their claim to equal worth on the basis of their own merits. So the enemy was first and foremost the inertia and lethargy among the dormant victims. The counterweapons were the pamphlets and flimsy little newspapers, the societies of mutual support and the untiring efforts to build one's own schools and lodges, or whatever other institutional means appeared available to hoist self-esteem and forge the socio-psychological mold of what--again in reference to nineteenth-century Europe--has been called the Mentality Class.

Once this crucial stage had been reached--when the group as a whole had become conscious of the burden imposed upon it by the inherent structures of dominant society--the movement changed pace and momentum. It grew in numbers and scope and branched out into an increasing diversity of points of view; this resulted in fierce internal debates. Common deprivation does not imply a consensus of opinion about the goals to be achieved or the roads that lead to them. All sorts of different approaches began to find expression and vie for allegiance. Some stressed the need for cultural self-assertion or preached moderation and restraint, trusting to individual accomplishment and the favor of the larger society; others opted for more militant forms of action, advocating political alliances or purely economic organizations as a means of exerting pressure. Others encouraged even more drastic solutions, including physical violence or massive obstruction, thereby indicating their distrust of anything short of total social revolution. Illustrations abound for each of the four movements.

Among America's ethnic minorities some concentrated on fostering traditional values through neighborhood organizations and parochial schools, thus laying the foundation for those individual and collective qualities that would further social mobility. But there were also those who entered aggressively into the economic and political power struggle, creating labor unions and ward clubs designed for getting out the vote, taking over offices, or establishing monopolies (which at times involved criminal extortion practices or the application of mob tactics). Indonesia's nationalists championed indigenous education, religious revival, or economic cooperatives, but also engaged in coalitions based on political expediency; or they argued against such collaboration and, instead, chose a course of civil disobedience, which on one occasion erupted into open rebellion (the abortive revolt of 1926). Holland's Roman Catholics were perhaps exceptional in that--especially in the eyes of the outer world--they demonstrated great cohesion and closed ranks in a tight network of para-formations on a strictly confessional basis. Nevertheless, even they showed a wide range of opinions concerning the most effective ways to overcome the complex obstacles that separated them from their goal--crushing Protestant dominance and stemming the tide of rising secularist doctrines, whether liberalist or socialist. Finally, the European labor movement, almost from the very beginning, found itself deeply divided over issues of social philosophy, policies, strategies, or priorities, and as a result split into a myriad of factions often more intent on defeating one another than on confronting the common enemy.

From this _mêlée_, however, major alignments gradually emerged. They would eventually become decisive factors in determining the future course of the movement. At a certain point, definite emphases developed that were finally to force a resolution, either in terms of assimilation or transformation. Internal confusion and collision evolved into a polarization of clearly alternative positions. The strength of constituencies as well as social conditions had crystallized enough to suggest the viability of different approaches. This is not to say that rival interests did not continue to hold sway over larger or smaller numbers of devotees; such groups often survived for a long period of time, until or even beyond the moment when the original movement reached its final stage, and so formed the nucleus of new potential movements. A dominant center of gravity became apparent, suggesting the basic way in which the emancipation process would achieve its optimum objective.

In the case of the European labor movement, both the advocates of a cautious policy of reformist liberalism and the left-wing extremists promoting all-out revolution through strikes, class-war, or creation of total chaos, steadily lost ground to the radical opportunists. The latter, though committed to a militant socialism, exploited to the fullest whatever leverage they could lay their hands on to bring about fundamental change within existing social institutions. Broadly-based and well-disciplined workers' unions pressed for tangible economic improvements. They also operated in close alliance with political parties that besieged governmental and legislative strongholds and continuously battered the walls of the status quo, taking advantage of every opportunity. The Dutch Roman Catholics, in turn, struck a similar balance--between inclusive confessional self-organization and fragmentation into separate groups. While valuing separatist, religious solidarity, they still joined in various coalitions on particular occasions when common wounds could be assuaged through united agitation. Therefore, in matters of educational autonomy, they sided with orthodox-Protestants; in matters of social and economic justice, with the militant fighters for the proletarian cause; in matters of political representation, with those in favor of popular democracy.

To a limited extent, the same applies to the ethnic minority groups in the United States. They relied increasingly on the pooling of their voting strength, the value of education and independence in the development of socio-economic resources, and the appeal to the ideal of individual initiative inherent in the image of the dominant society. The result was a weakening of the attraction of nationalist rallying-cries and forcible tactics that yielded to a gradual process of partly collective, partly individual integration into the mainstream of white America.

Quite different, on the other hand, was what occurred on the Indonesian scene. Here, the proponents of collaboration remained for a long time locked in an uneven battle with non-collaborationists. As long as the colonial administration stayed securely in charge, gradualism and phased concessions appeared to be the only feasible alternative to vigilantly checked subversion or jail. But when World War II precipitated the collapse of Western colonialism, the odds began to favor those who had shunned any compromise with the faltering regime. A zealous drive--including opportunist power deals with foreign forces of a hardly less detested, imperialist character--was directed toward complete national independence, devoid of special ties to the "mother country," and fashioned according to indigenous concepts of communal corporatism or democratic collectivism.

By these routes, then, each movement gained sufficient momentum to establish itself eventually as a major component--if not the dominant one, as in the Indonesian case--of the larger society. At that point the final stage was reached, ending the life-cycle, the subsequent stages of which can be schematically summarized as follows:

EMANCIPATION MOVEMENT INTERNALLY

Life-Cycle Stages

1	2	3	4	5
"Situation Class"	"Mentality Class"	Internal Confusion/ Polarization	Major Thrusts' Break-Through	Consummation

The movement's consummation also implied a change in the enveloping order, either by integrating the emancipated element into its fabric, or by itself becoming transformed to some degree.

Emancipation Movement Vis-À-Vis the Society and its Response

Having considered the emancipation movement's internal dynamics, the next logical step is to examine its external aspects. Movement never occurs in a vacuum; it necessarily unfolds within a wider context. Social movements emerge and evolve in relationship to the surrounding society, which in turn reacts to them. Consequently, this process needs to be studied from a dual perspective: the movement in action and society reacting. Since both perspectives, although clearly distinct, are actually as closely related as challenge and response, they are dealt with simultaneously in this section, and identified as the M(ovement) ⟶ S(ociety) and the S(ociety) ⟶ M(ovement) perspectives, respectively.

From the M ⟶ S perspective, the earliest action consisted of a more or less explicit appeal for sympathy and help. This appeal generally elicited--when considered from the S ⟶ M point of view--a twofold response. On the one hand, it was met by either spontaneous or organized acts of charity. Philanthropy was the conditioned reflex by which the more enlightened among the elite attempted to address the needs of the underprivileged. This was the traditional way of alleviating immediate emergencies, even though such emergencies seemed to possess a new quality, requiring additional measures. On the other hand, there was also the equally traditional tendency on the part of the more conservative, to be shocked by what they felt to be rather impertinent demands. On the whole, however, neither the growing restlessness of the victimized awakening to an understanding of their plight, nor the compassionate or vaguely alarmed counterimpulses generated in the society at large, had a clear focus. All this pointed to symptoms rather than causes; there was no real awareness of what was wrong, where to go, or what to do--only an instinctive feeling that the old established patterns were somehow wanting. The first reaction, therefore, was to submit petitions, show benevolence, or brusquely resort to stricter enforcement of those rules that heretofore had governed relations with the dependent.

Eventually, however, a shift occurred. Respectful pleas took on a defiant note; deeply imbued habits of dependence on the benignity of the powerful and well-to-do gave way to a growing consciousness that "rights" must be fought for. Greater stress was placed on self-reliance and solidarity with others similarly deprived. This found clearest expression in the case of the poverty-stricken, whether they were European proletarians or American first-generation immigrants. In their plight--exaggerated by unprecedented conditions of urban overcrowding and economic vulnerability--they moved from hat-in-hand relief recipiency to the organized pooling of their own resources, agitating for their rights in alliance with groups of varying degrees of militancy. In the process, the mood of the poor was one of social criticism. Concern became widespread among the better-off. A few became aware of the existence of real suffering that demanded new forms of private and public aid; others, unable to understand, felt insecure and threatened, and so were tempted to resist, reprove and even retaliate. Acts reflecting an emerging "social conscience" (individual citizens experimented with social and economic projects however paternalistically conceived; or social legislation to prevent abuses in child and women's labor were initiated) existed side by side with expressions of heightened discrimination and repression.

This applies, mutatis mutandis, both to Holland's Roman Catholics and to Indonesia's nationalists. For instance, the former succeeded in gaining support for ecclesiastical and educational self-determination, as witness the official restoration of Dutch Roman Catholic dioceses in 1853, and the legal establishment of confessional schools in 1857. But the Dutch Roman Catholics also ran into the aroused opposition of Protestant "anti-papists" (April movement of 1853) and the obstructive inflexibility of the liberalist "secularists"--which in turn led to a rash of demonstrations uniting Roman Catholics, orthodox Protestants, and anti-clerical Socialists in a common assault on the established order (culminating in the universal suffrage campaigns of the 1880's). On the other side of the globe, in colonial Indonesia, nationalists of all types--including Indo-Europeans caught in the ambiguities of their "marginality"--were successful in eliciting from the authorities a commitment to social and cultural "uplift" and to distant promises of home rule; at the same time they faced a resurgence of the "white man's burden" arrogance and a clamor for police-state vigilance.

Eventually, a situation evolved which, from the M ⟶ S perspective, presented a picture of chaos and confusion. The emancipation movement, internally fragmented into many feuding factions, had reached the stage at which both radicals and moderates, adherents to pure principles and pragmatic realists, sought to win over the masses to their reppective targets and tactics. On the other hand, from the S ⟶ M perspective, the forces of support and resistance had also arrived at an impasse. In a word, a double breaking-point was imminent. The status quo began cracking under the severe--although still erratic--pressure of a diversity of forces for change. As a result, the existing order was confronted with a basic decision for or against structural responsiveness. And when finally the break-through occurred, both the movement and the dominant elites experienced a crystallization of options that led either toward a total polarization of extreme demands versus rigid conservatism, or opened up new avenues for give and take. At this point a decision had to be made: whether the emancipation movement would collapse under the weight of powerful counterforces, explode into all-out revolution, or continue its course as a movement for change, achieving its goal without actual revolution. As indicated before, we are dealing here with the latter possibility only--that is, a situation in which the forces of gradual rapprochement were stronger than those of total polarization; and consequently an evolutionary rather than a revolutionary development led eventually to a substantially altered state of affairs.[2]

Clear cases in point can be found in many nations of western Europe that went through periods of great turbulence in the late nineteenth and early twentieth century, due to fierce agitation of all sorts by all sorts of minorities, be they women, proletarians, or citizens who were considered second-rate because of creed or some other anomaly. In all these nations this commotion ultimately shaped new alignments. Those unwilling to compromise lost out to those who gradually joined forces. This was particularly evident in the labor movement's struggle over the issues of "revisionism" and "parliamentarism" on the one hand, and on the other, the establishment's growing rift between those opposing and those supporting the necessity for reconstruction. Part of this development in the Netherlands was the Roman Catholic drive for emancipation. Their separatism at first provoked strong sentiments for containment, yet it eventually took a direction that proved flexible enough to gain allies in their fight for full citizenship.

The American scene can be described as different in detail, but essentially similar. Here, the ethnic immigrant groups had internal battles that pitted all-or-nothing zealots against the advocates of a more pragmatic approach. In the process, they encountered an often violently expressed "nativism," as well as honest efforts to act in the best traditions of this land of the free. The long-term trend, however, was toward a phased integration into the mainstream of society which, by a continuous process of moves and countermoves, absorbed the newcomers. Their swelling numbers and diligent energies produced coveted partners in the complex coalitions of "machine" and "reform" elements, typically exemplified in the ascendant Democratic Party. Only in the case of the Indonesian nationalist movement did the final stages take a different form. There, conditions were not propitious for an evolutionary process but built up to a revolutionary confrontation between a colonialism that failed to heed the signs of the times and an unbending determination to achieve absolute, national independence. Consequently, the following diagrams, which attempt to summarize the successive life-cycle stages described above, require different characterizations for the Indonesian development in its later stages:[3]

EMANCIPATION MOVEMENT EXTERNALLY

From M ⟶ S Perspective

1	2	3	4	5
Appeals to Establishment	Mixed Coalitions on Self-Help Basis	Breaking-Point: Purists vs. Pragmatists	Gaining Participation (waning Extremism)	Co-determination

From S ⟶ M Perspective

1	2	3	4	5
Philanthropy versus Growing Backlash	**Supportive Paternalism**	**Breaking-Point: Liberals vs. Conservatives**	**Dawning Realization of Change (withering Backlash)**	**Assimilation Transformation**

NOTES AND REFERENCES

Chapter V

1. We follow here the terminology of the Dutch sociologist J. P. Kruyt, whose concepts of Situation and Mentality Class (toestands- and mentaliteitsklasse) cover the distinctions which Marx--in his Das Elend der Philosophie--made between Klasse an sich and Klasse für sich. It should be noted that the English translation "Mentality Class" means to convey what the Dutch word mentaliteitsklasse includes; that is, it indicates the psychological dimension of having become conscious of one's situation. J. P. Kruyt, "De sociale structuur ven het Engelse volk," Tijdschr. Kon. Ned. Aardrijkskundig Genootschap, 1937, p. 841.

2. See p. 46 above. As has been and will be shown, an exception should be made regarding the Indonesian nationalist movement which could not achieve its final goal of national independence without actual revolution.

3. In stages 4 and 5, the Indonesian nationalist movement was typified by a Suspended Balance of Cooperatists and Non-Cooperatists/ Prevailing Conservatism (rather than Gaining Participation/Dawning Realization of Change) and Complete Take-over (instead of Co-determination).

PART THREE:

THE MOVEMENT AND THE UNITED STATES -- WHERE ARE THEY HEADING?

> If ever the free institutions of America are destroyed, that event may be attributed to the unlimited authority of the majority, which may at some future time urge the minorities to desperation, and oblige them to have recourse to physical force.
>
> Alexis de Tocqueville[1]

CHAPTER VI

FROM "RIGHTS" TO RADICALISM: THE "MOVEMENT" IN TRANSITION

One thing becomes clear when viewing the United States movement of the 1960's from the perspective of earlier emancipation movements that have completed their development. It is impossible to give an unequivocal answer to the question of where this movement, as it has developed over the last decades, fits into the typological construct of the Assimilation/Transformation continuum. This is perhaps a logical consequence of the breadth of definition to which the present study subscribes: the Negro fight for full citizenship, the young protesting the threats of an emerging "technopolitan" society. This inclusive understanding seems to make it a foregone conclusion that the United States movement had acquired an additional dimension.

However, this raises the question of whether this inclusiveness is contrived or real. In our opinion, the evidence strongly suggests the latter. The new style which, in the very first pages of this volume, was stressed as being particularly distinctive of the movement of the 1960's, cannot possibly be regarded as the product of clever manipulation or scholarly juggling. On the contrary, there can be little doubt that what occurred in recent years is exactly what constitutes the true nature of an emancipation movement. Such a movement may start out focusing on the immediate concerns of a well-defined group suffering from a specific form of victimization. But its programmatic push propels it far beyond that initial area of concern to touch upon issues fundamentally affecting the whole of society. What actually happened was that the movement highlighting the particular plight of the Negroes' inequality in American society--which established it as a movement for civil rights in the strict sense--turned increasingly into a thrust requiring that society _per se_ to face the general problem of human rights.

From Civil Rights to Human Rights, 1954-1968

These dates (1954-1968) represent an approximation, but they serve a definite purpose. They make it clear that the development in question is uniquely characteristic of a distinct period in contemporary American history. It is the period which roughly coincides with the fourteen-odd years that elapsed between the Supreme Court's momentous school desegregation decision and the Riot Commission Report's exposure of "white racism."

At first sight, this may seem puzzling. What is so unique about this brief span of time which seems only another episode in the long and tragic sequence of events that has been unfolding ever since the day the American Negro was formally declared a free man? The facts suggest how little real difference exists between recent and past developments. Thus, in an essay entitled "What Happened to the Civil Rights Movement," published early in 1967, C. Vann Woodward wrote:

> Students of Negro life in America have enjoyed some rare opportunities over the last dozen or so years. As if adopting the techniques of cinema, history has obligingly thrown in a succession of flashbacks or replays of hauntily familiar lines, encounters, whole episodes from the past. It would seem at times, in fact, that contemporary history has been plagiarizing an old scenario and helping itself to the script.[2]

This noted historian speaks of the post-1954 resurgence of the Negro's century-old liberation struggle as "the Second Reconstruction," and points to specific analogies and parallels to what occurred during and after the First Reconstruction that followed the Civil War. Striking parallels abound. New statutes and court rulings are nothing new, nor are the half-hearted or sabotaged attempts at implementation; efforts at improvement through education and economic advancement, and acceptance into the society's mainstream by integration, are as familiar as rebuffs, whether subtle or direct. Even strong attempts to assert "black identity" through cultural nationalism and political separatism are a common phenomenon in the Negro movement of the 1920's and 1960's, if not as early as the 1860's.[3] In brief, the similarities are too obvious to be ignored, and the dissimilarities seem to be a matter of degree rather than of principle.

Nevertheless, C. Vann Woodward did not hesitate to put full stress on significant "contrasts in style, temper, and rhythm." The situation _is_ different, and this he considered due particularly to:

> two distinctive features of the Second Reconstruction: (1) the predominance of the Negro, and (2) the predominance of youth. This helps explain why it was more spontaneous and less contrived, more improvised and less premeditated. It had a wild, untamed exuberance baffling to the older generation. Paternalists and philanthropists of the Establishment, black and white, not only lost control, they often lost touch. They were not _with_ it. In the theme song of the revolution the verb "overcome" was intransitive but, had it taken the transitive form, one of the objects of "to overcome" would have been "the older generation." For this was in part a generational rebellion that cut across racial lines and transcended racial objectives.[2]

These few lines state in a nutshell the case to be presently elaborated. They strongly support the notion that the Negro Civil Rights Movement--while apparently repeating the same cycle of slow progress and subsequent repulse which marked it for almost 100 years--has definitely shifted gears in the last two decades. The full impact and real nature of this change, however, is only partially explained by the two distinctive features noted by Woodward. To be sure, he correctly points to such salient phenomena as the wider, more mass-based and increasingly grass-roots involvement of the Blacks themselves, and the intensely dedicated participation of large numbers of young activists who have proved time and again their willingness to bear the brunt of the battle. It is beyond question that these factors accounted in no small measure for the far greater drive and radicalized tone of the movement. Nevertheless, one is left with the impression that the movement, however broadened in support and quickened in temper, was still basically concerned with the central issue of the Negro's civil rights--and it is precisely this interpretation which strikes us as insufficient.

It is perhaps only fair to state that at the particular time when Woodward made his observations--in late 1966--it was virtually impossible to have a clear perception of what was actually stirring. History moves fast nowadays; what today appears as a pattern of occurrences suggestive of significant change had hardly begun to surface yesterday when no one could definitively identify a new trend from the scattering of unrelated incidents. Thus the present author readily admits that his own understanding of the United States movement has changed substantially during the years between the middle 1960's and the closing days of that decade. The new momentum, so clearly discernible since the 1950's, could easily have been explained in relation to the worldwide wave of decolonization which sharply heightened the sense of solidarity among all colored people. The equally evident overtones of economic unrest, youthful protest, and impatience with paternalism and do-goodism, could likewise be viewed in the context of the revolution of rising expectations that affected the emerging "developing countries." At the same time, all this added impetus to the defiant idealism of a new generation questioning the rigidity of established dichotomizations.[4] In short, by about 1966 the movement's fresh zeal and vigor appeared to be only a domestic concomitant of the great reawakening of the ex-colonial Third World with its newly gained independence which filled all men of color with pride.

But, since then, it became increasingly evident that the civil rights, or Negro, issue could not be separated from a range of other issues that deeply disturbed America's inbred belief in the perfectibility of a way of life founded on the rule of law and committed to the pursuit of happiness. Especially since 1965--the year in which the fury of Watts followed less than six months after the euphoria of Selma's symbolic victory of non-violence in the face of repression--this belief had been dealt blow after blow. Three developments in particular need to be mentioned, involving some of the most dramatically significant events in the brief but incredibly emotion-packed period from early 1967 to late summer 1968:

	URBAN CRISIS	VIETNAM WAR	YOUTH ALIENATION
Spring 1967	Early start of the "long hot summer" of urban unrest	Martin Luther King publicly joins anti-war mobilization in recognition of inseparability of freedom, justice and peace in the struggle for human dignity	
Summer 1967	Nationwide urban violence; Kerner Commission instituted		Hippie communes congregate at the big cities' Haight-Ashburies
		National New Politics Conference rallies radical opposition, calls for grass-roots organization and direct action against entrenched Establishment politics; and accepts Black Power bloc as entitled to 50 per cent of the vote on all decisions on the floor	
Fall 1967		Sen. Eugene McCarthy enters Presidential campaign and evokes strong support from the young for his anti-war and party-reform position	
Winter 1968		Tet offensive shatters peace by military victory myth	
Spring 1968	Kerner Report exposes "white racism" in U.S. society	President Johnson announces deescalation, and "abdicates"	Widespread student revolts abroad and at home
	Assassination of Dr. Martin Luther King followed by outburst of urban ghetto rage		
Summer 1968	Senator Robert Kennedy assassinated		
		Democratic Convention disorders and police "overreaction"	

(1) The first development was the sudden confrontation due to the devastating evidence of urban rot. For some time an uneasy awareness had been spreading among those who had experienced the adverse effects of sprawling high density concentrations. Yet it took the unprecedented furor of the Watts explosion, in August 1965, to shock an urbanized America into a realization of the gaping rents in the metropolitan milieu. But even Watts, however stunning its impact, still did not produce a full appreciation of the destructive forces at work in urban America. What it did create was a dawning consciousness of the Negroes' condemnation to a ghettoized existence in inner cities tightly sealed off from the opulence of lilywhite suburbia. Nevertheless, it required the trauma of a nationwide outbreak of race riots--on a limited scale in 1966, but all-out in 1967--to force society at large to recognize its own responsibilities for the ailing metropolis. It was this experience which instigated the President's National Advisory Commission on Civil Disorders, and thus set the stage for a painful probe into the causes of the violent urban crisis. And it was this probe which revealed mainstream America's collective guilt in creating, maintaining, and condoning an inherently unjust social and political order, built on institutionalized inequities and deeply-rooted

segregationist practices. Like a thunderbolt, the ugly truth struck the nation's conscience: at the heart of the societal breakdown was not the black man's alleged inability to qualify for the American way of life, but rather the pervasive insidiousness of "white racism" which legalizes injustice and rationalizes the systematic denial of equality. In other words, what occurred was analogous to what evolved in nineteenth and early twentieth century western Europe. The "problem of poverty" soon became identified as the "labor question," or the core issue of the proletarization of the working classes. This, in turn, led eventually to the admission that "the social question" was the dehumanization perpetrated by a ruthlessly individualistic, profit-oriented, industrialized capitalist system.[5] Similarly, in contemporary America, the "Negro problem" became the wedge which split open the long-cherished delusion of the melting pot, and disclosed the fundamental division in American society. Through the dramatic convulsions of the urban crisis, the issue of race betrayed at long last its real nature--the blindness of the majority to its own "racist" arrogance; the black man's plight boomeranged in a society that defined its promise of freedom and opportunity exclusively in terms of the white man's dominance.

(2) In addition to the violent eruption of the urban issue on the domestic scene, there was the agony of America's foreign entanglements. This crisis resulted from the country's involvement in the dilemmas of anti-Communist world leadership and its attempt to bolster the shaky foundations of indigenous nationalist regimes. The problem became particularly acute in the years following the decision of the Johnson Administration early in 1965 to commit massive military forces to the Vietnam conflict. The war escalated and soon plunged the nation into a state of disarray which testified to the utter confusion of its priorities. In 1966, the Senate's Foreign Relations Committee began to raise the question of America's policy of usurping power by proclaiming itself the protector of the world's freedom. Freedom was equated with whatever America took, or mistook, for its national interest. The war coincided with manifestations of a grave domestic crisis in the cities and between the races, making a growing number of people wonder about the warped sense of values that allowed an arms' budget to spend five times the allocation for emergency measures to offset the effects of poverty. As a result, a "credibility gap" developed which created, especially among black militants and young white radicals, a desperation that found expression in vituperation, separatism, and revolutionary resistance. Yet the full extent of this gap was not really apparent until Dr. Martin Luther King risked the great moral prestige he enjoyed among "responsible" and "reasonable" Americans, both black and white, by openly linking the civil rights cause with the Vietnam issue. Judging from the public commotion following this move, even Dr. King's committed supporters appeared embarrassed. They considered the move ill-advised on the part of this noble advocate who had unfailingly appealed to the nation's basic decency in the struggle against the unconstitutionality of segregationism. In April 1967, The Washington Post editorialized: "Many who have listened to him with respect will never again accord him the same confidence"; while The New York Times deplored "Dr. King's Error," which consisted of his "fusing of two public problems that are quite distinct and separate."[6] One year later, however, the force of events shockingly revealed the indivisibility of the problems, hastened

the end of a presidential career, and precipitated political murders. The erosive effects of military escalation and racist polarization confronted the country with the brutal reality of a way of life infested by violence and haunted by fear and frustrations.

(3) At this point the increasing radicalization of the youth became manifest. Their revolt was a characteristic part of the broad wave of protest, dissent and discontent which has marked the 1960's from the beginning. Youth had predominated in the Freedom Movement since the earliest sit-ins, in the anti-war and non-intervention campaigns since Castro's victorious Cuban guerillas, as well as in the drive for reform on and off campus since C. Wright Mills' writings fathered the New Left intellectuals-for-social-change. Then apparently around the middle of the decade, a significantly new tone and intensity began to surface. The Berkeley Free Speech Movement of late 1964 was clearly representative of the new turn: the various issues that triggered the concern and involvement of many young activists suddenly seemed to fuse and seemed to be inextricably interrelated. Mario Savio articulated this when he spoke of "the two battlefields" of Mississippi and Berkeley:

> The same rights are at stake in both places--the right to participate as citizens in democratic society and the right to due process of law. Further, it is a struggle against the same enemy. In Mississippi an autocratic and powerful minority rules, through organized violence, to suppress the vast, virtually powerless, majority. In California, the privileged minority manipulates the University bureaucracy to suppress the students' political expression.[7]

The trend which surfaced at Berkeley became ever more apparent in subsequent years. On scores of campuses all over the nation protest demonstrations turned into increasingly bitter confrontations centering around a wide variety of specific issues--Vietnam or the draft, defense contracts or real estate policies, black studies or the hiring and firing of faculty. But underlying all these different points at issue was one all-pervading sentiment: disgust with a "system" so riddled with oppressive authoritarianism, so insensitive to the needs of those it allegedly serves. A deep sense of moral outrage and alienation made itself felt. Feelings of alienation ranged from cynicism about the futility of reform from within, to distrust of electoral politics as a hoax perpetuating a "Herrenvolk democracy,"[8] to full-fledged resistance and disruption aimed at bringing down the power elites. The eruptions at Columbia University--coinciding with the French students' Revolt of May 1968--were a single, though unmistakable, case in point. However, perhaps the disaffection, the turning-off, found even clearer expression in the "Hip" or "underground" culture revolution which burst into prominence in 1967. In that year, LSD became an instant fad and the love and flower children flocked by the thousands to the dorados of communalism that sprang up in the city streets and in the country. Since then the phenomenon perhaps has become less conspicuous, but certainly no less significant. A new life style emerged, signalling a critical departure from the prevalent norms of an older generation. As Martin Duberman has put it:

> One may loathe some of the ingredients (as do many of the young themselves), or argue that they have not yet (and

> never will) crystallize into anything distinctive enough to be called a culture, but though the mix be unpleasant, shifting and inchoate, if it continues to locate its center in the senses and emotions, in participation and sharing, in the unexplored, the spontaneous, the casual, the experimental, we may well be witnessing a decisive break with our society's hitherto dominant values of rationalism, puritanism, materialism and individualism.[9]

In sum, whether expressing themselves politically or "culturally," the young showed a radically escalated aversion to, if not rejection of, American society and the traditions to which they were heirs.

A First Conclusion: Integration Is Dead--Liberation Instead

In the light of these three developments, a more definitive conclusion can now be drawn with respect to the United States movement, and its location on the Assimilation/Transformation continuum. These developments leave very little doubt that the movement of the late 1960's was substantially different from that of the 1950's. Both in scope and focus, a dramatic change seemed to have occurred--away from assimilatory reform, toward a mood of transformative revolution, a change which represents a spectacular reversal of the movement's position on the typological continuum:

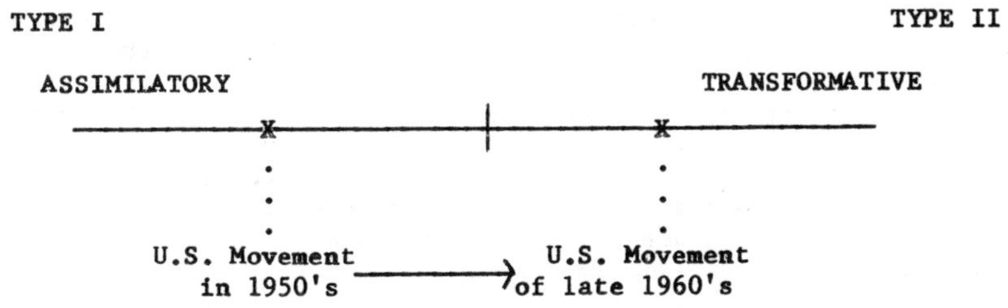

In spite of all its new vigor and drive, the movement of the 1950's, extending into the early 1960's, was limited to one issue and one goal: the factual segregation of and discrimination against America's black minority, and the fight for full citizenship in accordance with the inalienable rights granted in the American Constitution. Of course, other issues came to the fore, especially since 1960--Cuba, Vietnam, university reform, poverty. But they were completely overshadowed by the dominant concern for Negro rights. This was symbolized by the great momentum evolved under Martin Luther King's charismatic leadership since the days of the 1955 Montgomery bus boycott. This leadership combined a new mode of militant agitation with a passionately moral appeal to the nation's conscience. Massive campaigns of civil disobedience and passive resistance, rooted in a deep commitment to the philosophy of non-violence, inspired the many who had had no choice but apathy; they generated a new determination and audacious idealism especially among the young, both black and white, and . . . gained victories. New laws were enacted, abolishing restrictive practices or spelling out safeguards for effective enforcement, and legal battles were won in the courts. All this gave substance to a reborn hope that finally the old dream of one nation with liberty and justice for all might be approaching its fulfilment. In a word, integration was believed to be on the march.

Then, ensued the confrontation with the apartheid as practiced--regardless of what the laws stipulated--in the metropolitan centers of the north. Amid smouldering despair and sudden flare-ups of ghetto violence, the tactics of demonstrations and passive disruption still seemed to prove effective in dramatizing the issues and wresting concessions from city administrations. Yet, very soon it became clear that such concessions were Pyrrhic victories, producing official declarations of good intent but no results. A spectacular case in point was Chicago's so-called Summit Agreement on Open Housing of August 1966. After weeks of tumultuous marches, the city's top governmental and civic leaders met around the table with the movement's foremost representative, Dr. Martin Luther King. An eye-witness reported: "I have never seen so much power in Chicago in one room at one time! . . . And all of them were there to hear what the little brown man had to say"; but all that power evaporated into misty concepts, given the scorching climate of entrenched institutionalized discrimination. The conclusion was inescapable--the sickness underlying ghetto conditions in the nation's sprawling metropolises had produced a festering abcess of race and poverty, a symptom of a critical societal disease that required drastic surgery. The route of the law appeared to be a dead-end, and the goal of integration not only proved a phantom, but an odious one at that. What, in fact, did integration mean to the urban north? It was a composite of abundant statutes, ordinances, rules and rulings granting full equality to every citizen, on the one hand; and a cynical denial of that very right to equality, on the other. Society was involved in massive ghettoization under the cloak of fraudulent ideals. Integration, that is, assimilation into and acceptance by such a society, was seen to be a sick joke; first, because of the hollowness of the legal means to ensure it; and secondly, because this hollowness testified to the deeply ingrained double-standards governing the values and principles of the dominant society.

In that same year, 1966, the cry "Black Power" was raised for the first time and created great commotion and confusion among black and white alike. It rapidly established itself, however, as the symbolic expression of a radically altered mood, evidence of a thorough rethinking of the black man's position vis-à-vis American society in political, social, and--perhaps most of all--in psychological and cultural terms. Suddenly it seemed as though eyes were being opened to new realities of which, a few years ago, a man like Malcolm X had been the hard-hitting prophet:

> The word "integration" was invented by a Northern liberal. The word has no real meaning . . . it's a foxy Northern liberal's smoke-screen that confuses the true wants of the American black man. Here in these fifty racist and neo-racist states of North-America, this word "integration" has millions of white people confused, and angry, believing wrongly that the black masses want to live mixed up with

> the white man . . .
> Human rights! Respect as <u>human beings</u>! That's what America's black masses want. That's the true problem.
> The black man in North America was mentally sick in his co-operative, sheeplike acceptance of the white man's culture.
> The black man in North America was spiritually sick because for centuries he had accepted the white man's Christianity--which . . . had taught the black man to think if he had no shoes, and was hungry, "we gonna get shoes and milk and honey and fish fries in Heaven."
> The black man in North America was economically sick . . .
> The black American today shows us the perfect parasite image--the black tick under the delusion that he is progressing because he rides on the udder of the fat, three-stomached cow that is white America . . .
> The black man in North America was sickest of all politically. He let the white man divide him into such foolishness as considering himself a black "Democrat," a black "Republican," a black "Conservative," or a black "Liberal" . . . when a ten-million black vote bloc could be the deciding balance of power in American politics . . .[10]

The new reality of which Malcolm X spoke--and <u>for</u> which he spoke--was that of the seething black ghettos, packed with anger and a deep sense of degradation, loss of faith, and rejection by white America's middle class society. Not integration into that society, but <u>liberation</u> from it,[11] became the goal that the new leaders began to envision in terms of the existential needs of their new constituency. To the latter, the inhabitants of the large cities' sealed-off reservations of depression and frustration, survival was the immediate issue. It was an issue incomparably more tangible than the mirage of equality within a society in which they had neither part nor lot. To them, separatism was a bare fact of everyday life, which could be either endured in mute apathy or become the source of the defiant <u>will</u> to survive on their own terms.

For those whose lives are lived in virtual exclusion, separatism as a passive condition to separatism as a catalytic program is merely a step. This step has been taken before in the history of black America. The best-known instance of this is the Back-to-Africa Movement which, under the leadership of Marcus Garvey, spread the gospel of Black Nationalism in the 1920's. However, before and since then, similar movements have existed, ranging from Martin R. Delany's Pan-Africanism of circa 1860 to Elijah Muhammad's Black Muslims of a century later. Consequently, it would be a fallacy to consider the most recent variety of Afro-American nationalism or separatism, as expressed in the Black Power Movement, a uniquely new phenomenon. It certainly is not that--and yet a number of factors seem to suggest that there <u>is</u> something unique in the situation of the late 1960's. The "nationality strain" has been historically the "rejected strain," as Theodore Draper put it; after 1966, however, it became doubtful that the traditionally dominant "integration strain" in the thinking of America's black community was merely suffering a temporary setback.[12] The factors that can be cited are the following:

(a) As has been demonstrated, strong economic and social forces have created a vast concentration of black people in the inner cities of contemporary metropolitan America.[13] Never before had a concentration of such magnitude subjected black masses to a Lumpenproletariat existence on such a scale, in such a state of isolation.[14] Never before had the reality of black separateness been more starkly evident. The black ghetto had become a world in itself, with its own code and culture (including the "culture of poverty," to use Oscar Lewis's phrase), far removed from, and totally alien to, the rest of America's predominantly middle-class society. As a result, the message of integration into this society became an increasingly incommunicable one, and those carrying it faced oblivion as leaders.[15]

"The cold fact is that the Negro in America is not really in America," wrote Newsweek in a special report following the 1967 epidemic of urban riots.[16] Two years later, this same magazine published--as it had done twice before, in 1963 and 1966--the findings of a nation-wide survey of Negro attitudes. A substantial majority of those polled (all across the nation, in the south and the north, in cities as well as in rural areas) still appeared to favor integration and non-violent means; yet the indices of bitterness, alienation and independence increased significantly, as the following figures show:

	1966	1969
favor integration		63%
and non-violence,	59%	
but: latter is losing what it gained		52
reason can prevail,	51	46
but: progress is too slow	43	59
whites prove indifferent/hostile	54	69
sceptical of US Government stance (1966: LBJ; 1969: Nixon)	26	75
murder of Dr. King is a conspiracy,		82
which has never been fully investigated		67
police harmful to Negro rights,	33	46 (70)*
and their brutality is a fact		50 (58)
riots are helpful		40 (50)
and justified		31 (47)
agree: black is beautiful		74
blacks have special soul whites lack		54
black power	25 (31)	42 (68)
favor black nationalism/separate nation	5	21
and actually anticipate the latter		12

(*The figures between parentheses refer to the attitudes of those under the age of 30.)

(b) Not only was the black ghetto thought of as a distinctly separate world, subsisting on its own terms as a stigmatized, deprived and degraded caste, but also a new awareness of the American black man's condition emerged. The Negro saw himself as the product of the same colonialism that for centuries has governed the relationships between the white Western nations and the colored peoples they forced into servitude. This new awareness had a twofold aspect: on the one hand it was a clear expression of radical estrangement. The vast urban ghettos knew themselves to be as powerless and dependent (if not expendable) as any of the Third World's so-called developing countries. They are as much subjected by the overwhelming economic and technological dominance of outside forces. The following words, written by a Latin American about Latin America vis-à-vis the United States, might as well have been spoken by a resident of a North American inner city ghetto addressing himself to American society at large:

> The U.S. democracy is based on the principle that legislation--like taxation--without representation is unjust. But when an empire is built on an external proletariat, millions and millions of men are excluded from political representation, from making the decisions that concern them most. Their life or death, their human dignity or indignity, will be determined by what is called, with deadly precision, foreign policy . . .[17]

On the other hand, this awareness reflects a strong identification with and sensitivity to the defiant resistance characteristic of all decolonizing nations, as exemplified by China, Algeria, Cuba and, above all, Vietnam. If one lesson be learned from these nations, it is that no outside forces are powerful enough to shape a people's destiny once it has made up its mind to shake off the foreign shackles and become its own master. And this lesson <u>was</u> learned, most eagerly, in America's black ghettos. To illustrate this, one need only to mention a man like Eldridge Cleaver, whose <u>Soul on Ice</u> has been compared to the writings of Frantz Fanon. For both men "the central problem is of <u>identification</u> as a black soul which has been 'colonized' . . . by an oppressive white society that projects its brief, narrow vision of life as eternal truth"; a problem which led them to assume a position of militant resistance inseparable from the currents of world revolution.[18] Thus, in his angry essays, Cleaver returned again and again to this central theme: "We shall have our manhood. We shall have it or the earth will be leveled by our attempts to gain it." And this indeed has become the theme of the new ghetto breed. In cultural terms, it found expression in the almost obsessive preoccupation with the black man's indigenous--that is non-Western and non-white--identity, the roots of which were traced through a burning interest in African and Asian history and the learning of Swahili; experimentation with more or less syncretist forms of tribal or national religions; the sporting of "bush, beards, and beads" in addition to austere <u>nehrus</u> and colorful <u>dashikis</u>. Politically and economically, this theme recurs in the uncompromising demand that "control of the ghetto" be turned over to the people, not by what is considered the neo-colonialist gimmick of "black capitalism," but by reliance on schemes of self-help and self-government modeled after the socialist-communal orders of the nationalist type built by the Mao Tse-tungs, Ho Chi-Minhs, Nyereres, and other revolutionary leaders of the Third World. And in terms of tactics and strategies, it revealed itself in the explicit formulations of a <u>Black Manifesto</u> or the barely-veiled threats of "urban guerilla."[19]

In combination, these threats and demands disclosed the conviction that America's black masses possessed a moral right to large-scale "reparations," on pain of resorting to the only power they possess: the power to disrupt.

(c) Finally, there was the coincidence of the surging ferment of dissent among important segments of American white society. These segments, which previously tended to pin their hopes on the tradition of liberal reforms, now seriously questioned the viability of the American way per se. To them, the direction of American life was felt to be critically out of kilter. It had become a "system" of terrifying power, imposing itself both at home and abroad for the sake of stability, not liberty.

The word "coincidence" is an understatement. The radicalization of white critics, in particular the young, was inseparably related to the radicalization of the movement for Negro rights. A major thrust of the present study has been to demonstrate this fact. But others have labored this point as well. Thus, from his own black perspective, Eldridge Cleaver stressed the mutual impact of the two developments. He did so in global terms:

> . . . and just as world revolution has prompted the oppressed (colored nations) to re-evaluate their self-image in terms of the changing conditions (since World War II), to slough off the servile attitudes inculcated by long years of subordination, the same dynamics of change have prompted the white people of the world to re-evaluate their self-image as well, to disabuse themselves of the Master Race psychology developed over centuries of imperial hegemony.[20]

Cleaver was referring specifically to the rebellion of the white youth in the United States. He identified four general stages. First, in the 1950's, a growing disaffection with the prevalent conformity of booming American society became manifest in the deliberate anti-style of the beatniks. Then, circa 1960, the disenchantment began to turn from cultural withdrawal and political non-commitment to a more active search for roles to be played in confronting America with the revolutionary changes brewing inside as well as outside its borders.[21] (This was the period of the emerging campus unrest, coupled with agitation focusing on the Cuba question.) In the third stage, around the middle of the decade, the confrontation was sought chiefly through participation in the Negro struggle for integration, especially in the south. The fourth stage seemed to indicate that white youth, by applying the techniques learned from the Negro struggle, lashed out against society in general which they felt needed a total and radical reordering.

Cleaver's analysis, in other words, acknowledged that the white movement represented (a) a movement in its own right; (b) yet one deeply affected by the black movement whose catalytic impact transformed it into (c) a force that denounced American society as a whole. Thereupon, in this latter capacity, the white movement lent its aid to a further radicalization of the black movement. A case in point was the measure in which black militants of the Cleaver type at the time came to view the issue of race as a particular manifestation of a much more encompassing problem: that of a capitalist world order in which property rights take precedence over human rights. Toward the end of the 1960's, this broadened perspective clearly affected particular segments of the Black Panther Party whose revolutionary ideology--after having gone through an initial phase of reversed racism--appeared to be moving increasingly closer to the tenets of those New Leftists who were convinced of the inherent oppressiveness of the (American) capitalist system. Another instance of the converging militancy among whites and blacks was provided by the Vietnam issue. For a considerable time, the issue seemed to be of concern to whites only and black civil rights leaders grew suspicious of another "cop-out" on the part of their white supporters. By 1968 or 1969, however, the "hawk-dove" debate, or the matter of draft resistance, was no longer exclusively a preoccupation of the whites. For, as the 1969 Newsweek poll revealed:

> Negroes . . . have come to regard Vietnam as their own particular incubus--a war that depletes their young manhood and saps the resources available to healing their ills at home. The black backlash against the war is one of the most striking turnabouts since the 1966 poll: the notion that blacks ought to oppose the war because they have less freedom in the U.S.--a 35 per cent minority slogan then--has become a 56-31 majority sentiment today.[22]

A Second Conclusion: From Idealism to Ideological Battle

On the basis of the analytical patterns developed in Part II, there is a sequel to the first conclusion we had reached. In terms of the typological continuum pertaining to various historical manifestations of so-called emancipation movements, this first conclusion reads as follows: the United States movement of the late 1960's changed from a position near the assimilatory pole of anticipated change-through-reform to one much closer to the opposite pole, which is characterized by a desire for a revolutionary transformation of and radical break with the existing social order. This finding now raises a further question: what are the implications in terms of the life-cycle model--in particular insofar as this model concerns the internal development of emancipation movements, or their relation to society?

A first, tentative answer to this question follows from a point recurring in our discussion of the two specific dimensions of the life-cycle model: that is, the dimension dealing with the emancipation movement internally, and that focusing on the emancipation movement externally as viewed from the M(ovement) $\longrightarrow$ S(ociety) perspective. In this discussion, as one may recall, it appears that crucial decisions regarding an emancipation movement's future are likely to occur at one particular life-cycle stage. It is at stage No. 3, to be precise, that an emancipation movement enters what might be called the critical zone, in which it will be determined whether the drive for change can succeed at all; and if so, whether the conditions under which that drive takes place are such as to allow an assimilatory course, or are conducive instead to a transformative thrust--provided no all-out revolution results.

Considering this, it seems fair to assume that the United States movement of the latter part of the 1960's had arrived at the threshold of that critical zone, if in fact it did not go beyond it. Our conclusion concerning this movement's apparent radicalization suggests this by logical, though inverse, inference. If such indeed was the case--and we intend to demonstrate that it was--what then does it imply?

In order to explore further this matter, it may be worthwhile to return for a moment to that basic point of disagreement between Vann Woodward's assessment of the post-1966 state of The Movement and our own.[23] As indicated, we certainly have no quarrel with Woodward's poignant phrase of "the Second Reconstruction" insofar as it calls attention to the many parallels that were manifest in the more recent resurgence of the struggle for Negro rights in the United States, in comparison to earlier developments. Interpreting these parallels within the context of our life-cycle model, they lead us to the following conclusion: the long history of that struggle has largely been a repetitious process, characterized by a circular alternation of the same stages. At least twice before the new upswing of the Civil Rights Movement since about the mid-1950's, there has been clear evidence of progress from stage No. 1 to stage No. 2; but by the same token there has also been evidence of regression. Thus a book like W. E. B. DuBois' The Souls of Black Folk, which appeared in 1903, provides a wealth of material showing that the (first) Reconstruction days witnessed an unmistakable thrust in the direction of a new awareness and a growing sense of self-reliance.[24] Yet it is equally clear that this thrust, which is typical of the "Mentality Class"/Self-Help stage, suffered badly from the strong counterforces that in subsequent years put an abrupt end to the dawn of Negro freedom. The ideal of self-assertion, as raised and personified by Frederick Douglass, whom DuBois calls "the greatest of American Negro leaders," receded into a chimeric background. And what remained of it was Booker T. Washington's program of economic development and industrial training, which was being bought at the price (as DuBois remarks) of "submission and silence as to civil and political rights." A similar course of events is recorded in the chapters of Harold Cruse's The Crisis of the Negro Intellectual, which deal with the revival of that very ideal of black self-assertion in the years following World War I.[25] Once again powerful inroads were made on conditions of apathetic endurance and mute resignation characteristic of the "Situation Class" stage and the concomitant stage of Appeal to Establishment. A case in point is the stirring appeal of the Garvey Nationalists and the cultural renaissance which, at that time, turned Harlem into the undisputed "intellectual and artistic capital of the Negro world." In reference to the latter, Harold Cruse even goes so far as to say "that what was really at stake in the 1920's was what is today called Black Power . . ." But Cruse goes on to explain that this development stalled and disintegrated, due to the following two facts. First, the Garvey movement, which was predominantly a West Indian movement, did not really deal with the specifics of the internal United States situation but tended to see the solution to the Negro-white problem as a romantic escapism "outside the system--namely, in Africa." And secondly, the Negro intelligentsia never succeeded in ridding itself of the white middle-class standards that dominated both the cultural expressions of the Negro value system and their economic sponsorship--a failure which Cruse ascribed to the basic "racial integrationist premises" of the creative Negro intellectuals.

After these two abortive cycles it was not until the 1950's that a third round of the same process began to take shape. This time, however, the momentum and scope was markedly different--to such an extent that Vann Woodward spoke of significant "contrasts in style, temper, and rhythm," which he attributed in particular to "two distinctive features"; the predominance of Negroes and of youth. These features strongly suggest that something really new was now in the offing. This new element was that Negroes themselves, especially Negro youth, set the tone and pace of their struggle for equality and freedom--thus demonstrating an unprecedented independence from white liberals, whose partnership had always operated as normative leadership. This new phenomenon was significant indeed, if not full of foreboding. It meant that the life-cycle stage No. 2 now affected the United States black community on a scale that was far more extensive and intensive than ever before. In other words, apart from a mere quantitative difference, there also appeared a qualitative one, that is, a qualitative change of direction and intensity. And this implied in turn that, at long last, conditions were propitious for a further breakthrough, from stage No. 2 to stage No. 3.

In short, our hypothesis is that the situation of the 1950's was pregnant with consequences that had failed to germinate in earlier situations, during the 1870's and 1920's. Graphically put, this hypothesis can be presented as follows:

LIFE-CYCLE STAGES U.S. MOVEMENT

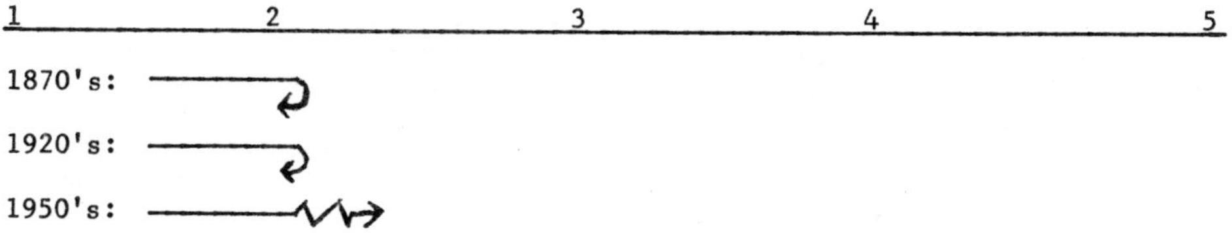

The imminence of that implied break-through in the 1950's certainly finds recognition in Woodward's comment that "this was in part a generational rebellion that cut across racial lines and transcended racial objectives." Yet, as we have said, Woodward did not seem to grasp the full import of what he had observed. (To which we must add, in all fairness: <u>how could he have</u> grasped it at that time? He did not have the benefit of the post-1966 hindsight we possess today.) What mattered was the movement's fundamental shift of focus from the central issue of Negro civil rights to the far more radicalizing one of human rights.

In retrospect, this shift could be traced to the messianic drive with which the towering personality of Martin Luther King implanted the moral imperatives of civil disobedience in the hearts and minds of his followers. The immediate issue at stake was the fight against the flagrant injustices inherent in southern segregationist institutions and life-styles. This fight was fought as a crusade for the sacred values of the Judeo-Christian tradition. It was a struggle of men of conscience, called to be witnesses to the supremacy of the law of God over the dictates of men. For as King put it in his <u>Letter from Birmingham City Jail</u>, which at times has the ring of Pauline writings conceived in similar surroundings:

> There are just laws and there are unjust laws. I would be the first to advocate obeying just laws. One has not only a legal but moral responsibility to obey just laws. Conversely, one has a moral responsibility to disobey unjust laws. I would agree with Saint Augustine that "An unjust law is no law at all." Now what is the difference between the two? How does one determine when a law is just or unjust? A just law is a man-made code that squares with the moral law or the law of God. An unjust law is a code that is out of harmony with the moral law. To put it in the terms of Saint Thomas Aquinas, an unjust law is a human law that is not rooted in eternal and natural law. Any law that uplifts human personality is just. Any law that degrades human personality is unjust.[26]

Grounded in such convictions, the movement of the 1950's and early 1960's struck at the deepest layers of America's founding principles. The Negro cause thus became the vehicle that would carry the nation back to its religious and idealist heritage. Past generations seemed to have forfeited this heritage. It had to be recovered by courageous and disciplined effort to reconstruct the social order in a manner in keeping with this nation's original principles.

Viewed against this background, it is understandable that in those days the movement transcended the racial issue, yet did not regard American society as basically incompatible with the ideal of human dignity. On the contrary, the strongest appeal rested on the belief that this society, in spite of all its flagrant deficiencies, could be made to live up to what it professed to be: the haven of the oppressed and the disinherited. Consequently, the all-out thrust was aimed at reform, although one spoke of reconstruction. These two terms are not contradictory; rather, they are synonyms expressing the same goal--to lead America back to its true destiny. This was the common perspective shared by both black and white who, standing shoulder to shoulder, demonstrated the possibility of fulfilling the American dream, with its promise of a truly integrated community.

However, this euphoric outlook was increasingly torn asunder as the movement moved north and confronted the harsh realities of the ghettoized metropolitan powder-barrels; it ran up against the devastating effects of the Vietnam issue, which became the focal point of a raging debate over the intrinsic nature of the nation's institutions and values. A proliferation of factions emerged, ranging from those clinging to a visionary belief in the ultimate integrity of the American experiment, to those who in profound disgust turned to esoteric ventures, or became agitators for a holocaust. As a result, the one-time unity of purpose, born of a multiplicity of motives, gradually dissolved into a mixture of ideological propositions whose protagonists sometimes seemed more intent upon battling one another than upon specifying the practical details of their respective blue prints.

Within the black community, this situation became manifest in the new flare-up of that old controversy between integrationists and advocates of separatism and nationalist, or--to use the current phrase --Black Power. Being an old controversy indeed, many aspects of the new flare-up clearly represented no more than a modern version of long-standing divisions. And yet, it would be a serious mistake to leave it at that. In our opinion, there are at least three significant differences that need to be taken into account in order to fully appreciate the direction of developments during the late 1960's.

(a) In the first place, the new divisions were not so much characterized by the fierceness of clashing positions, but rather by an unmistakable shift against the one position which in the past had always proven to be the predominant one. No doubt, on previous occasions, the integrationist position had often been under heavy attack as the level of frustration reached a peak among the black masses. However, time and again this frustration, which boosted the separatist position, receded as the aroused masses allowed themselves to be returned to the fold of those who continued to place their hope on the great American ideal.[27] But now it appeared that this hope had lost its appeal, and was rapidly being recognized as an illusion. The great American ideal itself was felt to be in disrepute; its postulate of the "open society" was fundamentally at issue in a society where even notable segments of the dominant majority were forced to admit that it was shot through with "institutional white racism" and "the arrogance of power." Consequently, integration was ideologically dead, and those still adhering to it found themselves in the extremely weak position of having no credible alternative vision. Without such a vision, their leadership became erratic; it lacked that most crucial, utopian dimension which transforms a social movement into an inspirational force that propels people beyond their frustrations and motivates them to move mountains. What remained was a powerless appeal to a drab realism which substitutes tactics for prophetic intransigence and passion.

(b) Secondly, there was another significant shift which further weakened the resilience of the "integration strain," while at the same time adding to the black community's state of internal confusion and polarization. In fact, it was a double shift reflecting both the erosion of the great American ideal and the new reality of vast concentrations of a black Lumpenproletariat in the big city ghettos. The latter reality --which is an unprecedented one in the history of Negro America--conditioned a constituency that created its own leadership. It was a leadership that could command allegiance only insofar as it gave expression to, and expressed itself in terms of the most immediate ills inherent in the daily experience of an underclass; its horizon was determined by its separation from the larger society--not as an ideological construct, but as a psychological and sociological fact. It was a leadership, in other words, of the primary level, locally based and highly charismatic in nature. Characteristic of this charisma was its competitiveness: it had to prove itself by demonstrating a superior ability in outdoing and outwitting "the enemy." In the prevailing atmosphere of growing political radicalization, this particular charismatic quality--which is the quality of the "hustler" so evident in the (auto)biographies of Malcolm X, Claude Brown, or Eldridge Cleaver--had two special consequences. On the one hand, it contributed to a broad spectrum of competing leaders, each claiming to offer the most effective approach in solving the problems and in changing unjust conditions. On the other, this entire spectrum of clashing views had one thing in common: it had its roots in the ghetto underclasses, and thus gave rise to a new black elite that posed a fundamental challenge to its traditional Negro counterpart. The latter's marks of distinction derived from the measure of success it had achieved in breaking away from its deprived condition and in adopting instead the middle-class norms of the white-dominated society. As a result, this traditional elite found itself caught in an agonizing dilemma. Not only was it confronted with the painful reappraisal of its position vis-à-vis the society that seemed to betray the dream that directed its life-long aspirations; but it was also faced with the psychologically even more threatening experience of being increasingly alienated from the broad base of its own people.

(c) Thirdly, there can be little doubt that this latter experience in particular could not but lend fresh impetus to that most significant trend already noted by Vann Woodward--the trend toward Negro predominance in the movement's leadership. This trend in itself was clear evidence of a new sense of identity stirring in the black community, a situation that completely altered prior black-white relationships. It expressed the dawning realization that the former relationship had never faced up to the gaping discrepancy between the premise of racial collaboration and the hard fact of an institutionalized racism that automatically subjects black people to a condition in which they "get defined, stigmatized, and rendered powerless by white people."[28] Given that condition, there could be no partnership save on terms that condemn the black man to a struggle without end. Whatever measure of success he may achieve, it is a measure beyond his control, because it has been predetermined by the values of the dominant culture. He can survive only at the price of negating the essence of his own manhood, to wit: the power to define himself. For this reason, the concept of integration, as the final goal of both black and white efforts, was bound to be seriously questioned. Even those who stuck to the ultimate validity of this goal, on the perfectly rational (and indisputable) grounds that self-propagated apartheid by a ten per cent minority amounts to political and economic suicide, could not overlook the equally indisputable counter-argument that this very goal offers no alternative but cultural emasculation. Thus a situation developed in which the issue of black power had to be squarely met by any one laying claim to a position of leadership in the movement. To be sure, not all were prepared to deal with this issue in the same manner, especially not when it first burst onto the scene in the early summer of 1966. Yet it is remarkable to see how soon the initial state of shock and embarrassment wore off, and made way for reactions characteristic of what might be called a bandwagon effect. Within a few months after Stokely Carmichael raised the cry, a subtle process of reinterpretation began to take shape. Progressively, it shifted from emphasis on the negative connotation of anti-white rabble-rousing to the positive one of black pride and self-esteem. In this latter sense, even the most committed champions of moderation were quick to pick up the slogan, to adapt it to the need to eradicate the Uncle Tom image, and to inject their following with a new vigor that would allow them to bargain as real partners. Even so, the ghetto-based militants kept pushing the issue by aggressively maintaining that their constituency's foremost interest did not lie in boosting their psychological self-respect, but in building a political and economic power base.

The conclusion to be drawn is twofold. On the one hand, it is quite obvious that the one-time dominance of the integrationist position was now being seriously challenged, both from within and without, by the powerfully emerging new theme of black consciousness. But on the other hand, it is equally clear that this new theme--which in itself marked a definite break-through--proved as yet too inchoate to establish an effective, new hegemony. What in fact prevailed was a multiplicity of points of view, all referring to a common rhetoric, but demonstrating so many shades and gradations of meaning that the resulting picture was one of utter fragmentation. It was a situation characterized by an apparent lack of leadership. Effective leaders were needed to overcome the paralyzing effects of disillusion with the old ideal of integration and to forge a binding alloy out of the diffuse elements of the new Black Power thrust. This thrust ran the gamut from complete racial separatism to cultural or political nationalism, to revolutionary Marxist-Leninism.

This sorry state of internal strife and confusion was perhaps even more evident among members of the movement's white wing. Here the combined impact of the radicalization manifest in all four major areas--race, poverty, war, youth revolt--had created havoc. The traditional liberal intelligentsia proved to be deeply split and disoriented. Their instinctive trust in the forces of "reasonableness" and the basic soundness of American life was being severely tested by the haunting awareness of devastating realities: institutionalized white racism, the Vietnam trauma, creeping pauperization, urban rot in the midst of super-abundance, and the generational fury against all middle-class values. Faced with this nerve-wracking experience, they were torn between half-hearted efforts to shore up reformism and the reluctant admission that American society had gone awry. The revolutionary transformations propounded by the New Left seemed justified. But the New Leftists themselves--old-line radicals plus a fresh crop of dissidents, equally scornful of the liberals' evolutionary creed--appeared to be divided in their ideological and strategic priorities. In this respect, _Fortune_'s special issue on American Youth of January 1969, provided pertinent information that seemed illustrative of the New Left's internal imbroglio.[29] An incredible diversity of styles, tactics and philosophies existed, that found expression in a horde of single- and multi-purpose organizations at all levels, and was forever prone to split into rival factions. And there were journalistic outpourings, some 200 of which then appeared, amounting to a total of over one million copies. One could only conclude that there was a complete lack of disciplined cohesiveness which, however, was found to be primarily due to a characteristic quality that, paradoxically enough, might well prove to be a distinctly new principle of union:[30]

> Philosophically, what seems likely to be most durable is the Movement's strong individualism and its quest for personal freedom. The Movement may someday be pulled together into a tightly structured, militant revolutionary organization--but it doesn't appear likely. All attempts to impose order or uniformity on it so far have failed. The fusion that _is_ taking place is between the political activists and the one-time hippie subculture, and that seems likely to create different "life styles" and ways of thinking in U.S. society, not a rigid political ideology.

By way of final summary, then, it seems fair to suggest that two salient points stand out in this bird's-eye overview of the major trends discernible in both the black and white components of the movement by the end of the decade. (1) Attendant to its radicalization (which, in schematic form, has been presented graphically on p. 75) the movement as a whole had apparently arrived at a stage close to the one which, in terms of the life-cycle model, marks a crucially decisive moment in the emancipation process. A new consciousness was emerging, which slowly revolutionized the optic angle of those in contention with the dominant society. It was an angle which evermore convincingly exposed that society as inhibiting the realization of man's inalienable identity. Yet at the same time, (2) it is very clear that this emerging consciousness had thrown the movement in great disarray. Nowhere was this more painfully reflected than in the waning of a once-respected leadership, whose defensive appeals to the commonly shared idealism of earlier days were increasingly falling on deaf ears, while a bewildering variety of challenging elites produced nothing but a cacophony of aggressive counter-themes.

What these two points amount to, in other words, is this: (a) When viewed internally, the United States movement of 1970 had proceeded beyond the life-cycle stage No. 2, the so-called "Mentality Class" stage, and thus found itself confronted with the agonies of "Internal Confusion/ Polarization" that are characteristic of stage No. 3:

LIFE-CYCLE STAGES, INTERNALLY

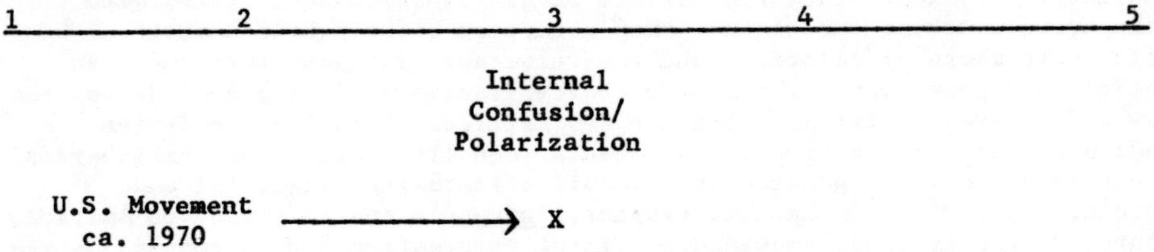

(b) Viewed from the M → S perspective, however, it should be stressed that the Movement now had arrived at the parallel stage No. 3, but to a certain extent only. Granted, there could be no doubt whatsoever that "purists" and "pragmatists" were very much in contention with one another; yet it was by no means clear when and how their struggle was going to lead to the "breaking-point" at which it becomes manifest who is taking precedence over whom in determining the future course of the movement:

LIFE-CYCLE STAGES, FROM M → S PERSPECTIVE

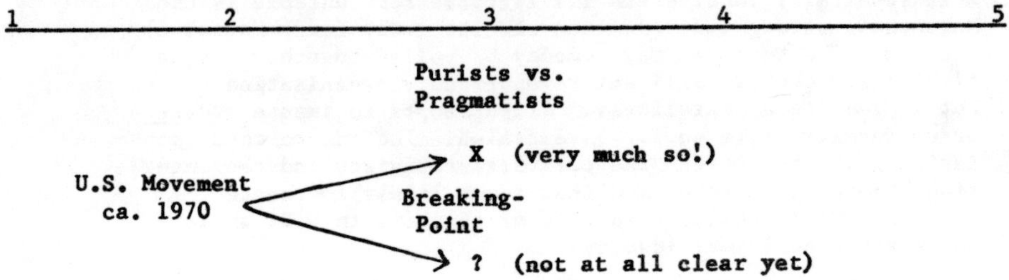

NOTES AND REFERENCES

Chapter VI

1. Alexis de Tocqueville, Democracy in America (New York: Schocken Books, 1964), Vol. I, p. 317.

2. C. Vann Woodward, "What Happened to the Civil Rights Movement" originally published in Harper's Magazine, January 1967, and reprinted in The Civil Rights Movement Re-examined (New York: A. Philip Randolph Educational Fund, 1968), pp. 11, 12-13.

3. The Harvard-trained physician Martin R. Delany (1812-1885) invented the slogan "Africa for the Africans" more than half a century before Marcus Garvey used the phrase according to Harold Cruse, who considers Delany the historical prototype of the Afro-American Nationalist. Harold Cruse, The Crisis of the Negro Intellectual (New York: William Marrow & Co., 1967), pp. 5-6.

4. In western Europe, for instance, many of the young critics agitate particularly against the inadequacy of their countries' response to the increasing economic and technological lag of the "poor nations" which, in their opinion, is a problem far outweighing the cold war considerations that led to the Vietnam quagmire.

5. Poverty/Labor/Social Question in Western Europe. P. E. Kraemer, The Societal State (Meppel/Holland: J. A. Boom & Zoon, 1966), Ch. II,3.

6. Public reactions to Dr. M. L. King's stand on Vietnam War. "Does Martin Luther King, Jr. have The Right? The Qualifications? The Duty? to speak out on Peace," sampling of press releases, editorials, rebuttals, letters to the editor, published and edited by Andrew Young, National Executive Director, SCLC (pamphlet, 1967).

7. Mario Savio and "the two battlefields" speech. Paul Jacobs and Saul Landau, The New Radicals (New York: Vintage Books, 1966), p. 230.

8. "Herrenvolk democracy," Pierre L. van den Berghe, in his Race and Racism (New York: John Wiley & Sons, 1967), defines a "Herrenvolk democracy" as "a parliamentary regime in which the exercise of power and suffrage is restricted, de facto, and often de jure, to the dominant group" (p. 29).

9. Martin Duberman, in The New York Times Book Review, March 23, 1969, p. 34, commenting on Christopher Lasch, The Agony of the American Left (New York: Alfred A. Knopf, 1969).

10. The Autobiography of Malcolm X, pp. 272, 312-313.

11. Liberation. Stokely Carmichael--being the first to raise the cry "Black Power," during the 1966 James Meredith March, as a battle-cry of electrifying quality--also contributed to popularizing the idea of "liberation" among U.S. militants, by subtitling his and Charles V. Hamilton's Black Power (New York: Vintage Books, 1967): "The Politics of Liberation in America."

12. Black Nationalism in U.S. history, Cruse, Crisis of the Negro Intellectual, pp. 4-6, 129. This same author quotes Theodore Draper.

13. See pp. 20-21 above.

14. Lumpenproletariat. This Marxian term, as applied to the black masses in today's U.S. metropolitan society, is well documented by Newsweek, in its November 20, 1967, issue, published under the overall title of "A Time for Advocacy."

15. As early as the first so-called "long, hot summer" (1964), The New York Times reported that Negro intellectuals realized that Martin Luther King could appeal to the upper and middle classes, but that Malcolm X alone could secure the allegiance of those at the bottom. To this, the following farsighted words were added: ". . . if Dr. King is convinced that he has sacrificed ten years of brilliant leadership, he will be forced to revise his concepts. There is only one direction in which he can move, and that is the direction of Malcolm X." As quoted in Alex Haley's Epilogue to The Autobiography of Malcolm X, pp. 417-418.

16. Newsweek, November 20, 1967. Newsweek surveys: issues of August 22, 1966 ("Crisis of Color '66") and June 30, 1969 ("Report from Black America").

17. Juan Luis Segundo, "Has Latin America a Choice?" America, February 22, 1966.

18. Maxwell Geismar, in the Introduction to Cleaver's Soul on Ice (New York: Dell Publishing Company, 1968), pp. xi, xiii.

19. Black Manifesto. Presented by James Forman in the spring of 1969 as an ultimatum to America's white churches, and stressing the concept of reparations due the U.S. black community for centuries of discrimination.

20. Cleaver on the white youth rebellion. Soul on Ice, pp. 69-75.

21. Advisedly, we add the facet of "political non-commitment" to Cleaver's characterization of the first stage. From our present-day

vantage point, it seems quite obvious that another, latent form of disenchantment played a part--however small and sub-consciously perhaps--in shaping the attitudes of the younger generation of the 1950's, whom Kenneth Keniston describes as The Uncommitted (New York: Harcourt, Brace & World, 1965).

22. Newsweek, June 30, 1969 ("Report from Black America"), p. 20.

23. See pp. 70-71.

24. W. E. B. DuBois, The Souls of Black Folk (Greenwich, Conn.: Fawcett Premier Book, 1967; orig. ed. 1903), esp. Essay II: "Of the Dawn of Freedom"; and Essay III: "Of Mr. Booker T. Washington and Others."

25. Cruse, Crisis of the Negro Intellectual, Parts I-II. The quotes are from pp. 82 ff.

26. Martin Luther King, Letter from Birmingham City Jail (Philadelphia: American Friends Service Committee, 1963), pp. 6-7.

27. It is on the basis of this "frustration reaction" that Bayard Rustin, one of the movement's grand old men, considers today's black power sentiments as understandable though unrealistic, as separatist spring-tides that developed in the aftermath of the Civil War and World War I. Bayard Rustin, "Toward Integration as a Goal," Separation or Integration--Which Way for America? A Dialogue by Robert S. Browne and Bayard Rustin (New York: A. Philip Randolph Educational Fund, October 1968), pp. 16-21. His position has even more emphatically been stated in his "The Failure of Black Separatism," Harper's Magazine, January 1970, pp. 25-34.

28. It is in these terms that J. Archie Hargraves refers to what he called "the Black condition," or "the contemporary form of the Afro-American experience." J. Archie Hargraves, You'd Better Listen, Mr. Charlie (UTC Pamphlet No. 2), p. 22.

29. Fortune, January 1969, "American Youth: Its Outlook is Changing the World," A Special Issue. Particular reference is made here to the contribution by Charles Burck, "Student Activists: Free-Form Revolutionaries," pp. 108-111, 134, 138.

30. Another significant indication that there was more than mere disunity follows from one of the main findings of an attitude survey, taken in October 1968 among a cross-section of college-educated youth, and reported in detail by Fortune. This finding reads that "behind the small and highly visible activist minority is a much larger and generally 'invisible' minority of forerunners holding similar dissident attitudes. It is in this forerunner group (making up about two-fifths of the student sample), a universe of some 2,300,000, that the problem of the generation gap is centered." Fortune, January 1969, pp. 67-69, 172-175 ("A Special Kind of Rebellion"), and pp. 70-71, 179-181 ("What They Believe"). See also Newsweek, May 11, 1970, pp. 24-28, "The Revolutionaries."

CHAPTER VII

TOWARD POLARIZATION--OR WHAT?

UNITED STATES SOCIETY AT A CROSSROADS

So far the focus has been almost exclusively on the movement proper, either in its internal developments, or in its stance vis-à-vis the larger society (that is, from the so-called M ⟶ S perspective). Now, however, full emphasis should be given to the question of how this larger society (from *its* S ⟶ M perspective) has been responding to the challenging presence of the movement in its ever-more intensified emancipatory thrust during the 1960's.

A response was inevitable. For emancipation movements are movements for change, striving toward a new order on the basis of a programmatic vision.[1] Hence, their first characteristic is that they no longer accept the status quo, but aim at changing relationships between the established classes and those who find themselves in a position of second-rate citizenship. From this follows a second characteristic: such action for change necessarily implies a twofold effect. On the one hand, it implies the effectuation of a change in the opinions and attitudes of established groups regarding second-rate citizens and their "traditional" place in the society. But on the other, it also implies the effectuation of a change in the behavior of the second-rate citizens themselves, since they must demonstrate that their behavior is no longer in keeping with that on which the established forces used to base their opinions and attitudes toward the emancipatory groups.[2,3]

Therefore, the findings of the preceding chapter are of particular relevance. They strongly suggest that during the second half of the 1960's, the movement made substantial progress in bringing about the latter effect. The growing appeal of black power within the black community, and the deep sense of alienation shown by radicalized young whites in their chaotic search for a new culture, could be seen as unmistakable evidence that the days of submissive and/or unquestioned subordination to the established order of things were over. In fact, what came to prevail was a rampant mood of defiance, serving notice that increasing numbers of Negroes-who-should-know-their-place were refusing to do just that, even as many of the nation's most privileged scions bruskly renounced the morality of the system in which they were raised.

In the face of this critical change, how then did the larger society react?

The Not So Silent Majority's Backlash

To all appearances, the response was the exact opposite of what the new militancy of the emancipatory groups supposedly should have accomplished. Instead of effecting a diminution in the dominant majority's negative attitudes to Negroes (let alone Blacks), or to white apostates from traditional American virtues, it appeared to have resulted in an intensified resentment and heightened hostility. This found expression in what might well be called a resurging populist wave of America's common-man-in-revolt, whose frustrations about the nation's alleged neglect of its most loyal citizens were vented in a great variety of ways. These frustrations undoubtedly had complex sources; yet it seems equally clear that the black revolution and the youth rebellion figured very large--both as underlying causes and as targets--in the surging backlash sentiments that became manifest among the rank and file of white America.

With respect to the race issue, it is evident that these sentiments had been building for several years. The deep strain of ambivalence characteristic of white attitudes became more pronounced than ever. This can be gathered for instance, from data supplied by the series of periodic surveys which Newsweek published on the subject during the 1960's.[4] Thus, in 1966, white Americans were found to agree, by more than 2 to 1, that "Negroes were discriminated against and deserved better"; yet at the same time, the victims of discrimination were increasingly believed to be overreaching themselves--as can be seen from the following comparative figures:

	1966	1963
"Negroes are trying to move too fast"	70%	64%
"Negroes are asking for more than they are ready for"	64%	54%

In 1969, whites still admitted--again by roughly 2 to 1--that "at least some of the demands presented by Negro leaders were justified"; but now there was an even stronger feeling that Negro complaints had but little basis in reality. Some 73 per cent, for instance, were of the opinion that blacks "could have done something" about slum conditions; 55 per cent felt the same way about the Negro unemployment rate; and nearly 80 per cent held that half or more of the welfare recipients (who are mainly thought of as blacks) "could earn their own way if they tried." In addition, the white respondents professed to believe--by great pluralities, as the following distributions show--that blacks in fact have an equal or better chance than people like themselves,

	better		or same		/ total
to get good housing at reasonable cost	35	+	27	=	62%
to get well-paying jobs	44	+	31	=	75%
to get financial help when out of work	65	+	22	=	87%
to get a good education for their children	41	+	41	=	82%

This last item is perhaps most significant of all--especially in view of the findings of three and six years earlier, when 54 and 41 per cent respectively of the sampling declared that "Negro children were receiving as good an education as white youngsters."

In brief, this data strongly points to a hardening, rather than a mellowing, of prejudice and ill-feeling. What caused this, however, was probably not so much the growing irritation with the ever-mounting pressure of black assertiveness but rather a nagging sense of insecurity now that it appeared as if all the old rules by which one attained accomplishments were crumbling. This latter anxiety certainly underlay the reactions to the youth rebellion in its political, and above all its cultural, manifestations. The challenge this rebellion posed was one that struck at the heart of white middle-class America's self-esteem. It was a challenge imperilling such treasured institutions as family, school, church; it eroded all the basic values one had lived by--the values of work and postponement of gratification, chastity and public prudence, filial deference and civic duty. What is more, it was a challenge laid down by those whom one had always cast in the role of examplars, the-kids-who-made-it-to-college, and with whom one identified as parents who had spent a lifetime of sacrifice. Hence, it was experienced as a direct threat to everything stable and right, a threat bitterly resented. This resentment was reflected in the 84 per cent of the 1969 Newsweek sampling who said "campus demonstrators had been treated too leniently"; or the nearly 60 per cent who could see "little or no justification for their actions." It was being voiced by the 70 per cent who considered that "people now were less religious than they were five years ago," and the 86 per cent who believed the nation's morals were being undermined by sexual permissiveness. And it resounded in the direct quotes of the average Marys and Joes, whose angry comments studded newspapers and magazines:

> I'm upset about the kids and the hippies and the absolute disregard for law and order and any kind of convention. It isn't the clothes. Hell, when I was a kid, I wore bell-bottom pants to school with silver bells on the side. But when I was the age of those hippies, I couldn't wait to get out and get a piece of capitalism and become part of the Establishment. But these kids grow up and don't want to be a part of it. That's what makes people mad. To these kids the future is nothing. To us, it was everything. It's sad. It's very sad.

> Everybody wants the same thing: decency. But people like us don't count any more. One woman can stop prayer in the schools. And a man with a prison record is patted on the head and told to do it again. Because Mr. Warren handcuffed our police, our laws are not protecting anyone.
> And the kids--they want it all right now, the things it took us a lifetime to get. A bath, a haircut, and a good old-fashioned strap would get most of them in line. But their mothers are too busy at cocktail parties and bridge clubs to be mothers.

As if this were not enough, there were additional concerns that were hardly less troubling. There was the unnerving problem of inflation sapping whatever personal prosperity had been gained; there were soaring taxes doing the same. There was a futile war abroad nobody understood, as mounting casualty lists brought the war closer and closer to home. And there was a malignant crisis in the nation's vast urban conglomerates where crime was rampant and the whole quality of life seemed to be in grave jeopardy. Consequently, it was small wonder that many succumbed to a grumbling sense of betrayal of everything they had held to be basic to this great country's foundations--with the inevitable result of a spreading malaise that was marked by psychological and political effects of an extremely ominous nature.

Psychologically, American society found itself rapidly torn asunder in two more and more alienated camps. A process of polarization became clearly manifest, showing distinct signs of escalation. An early case in point was the sharply divided opinions between whites (W) and blacks (B) on the basic causes of rioting, as revealed by a Louis Harris survey in August 1967:[5]

"the two or three main reasons" in respondents' own words	W %	B %	commonly cited causes considered major ones	W %	B %
outside agitation	45	10	police brutality	8	49
prejudice--promises not kept, bad treatment	16	36	lack of progress in giving equality	30	72
poverty--slums, ghetto conditions	14	28	lack of decent housing for Negroes	39	68
lack of jobs	10	29	lack of jobs	34	67

Similar contrasts were found to exist between dissident college students and those of comparable age groups who had not been to college. This came to light in many of the answers to the Fortune survey taken in October 1968.[6] It revealed--as the editors put it--"the extraordinary rejection of traditional American values" by about two-fifths of the students polled:[7]

	no college	dissident college
CURRENT ISSUES:	%	%
Feelings at stake in Vietnam war		
--patriotism	46	22
--strong support for U.S. position	46	14
Values always worth fighting for		
--fighting for our honor	64	20
--maintaining our position of power in the world	54	22
Draft resistance justified under any circumstances	17	67
Civil disobedience justified under any circumstances	18	66

Police action at Chicago Democratic Convention		
--not justified	26	60
--both sides were at fault	6	12
This country is doing too little for black people	35	71
HEROES, VILLAINS, AND IDENTIFICATION:		
Sense of solidarity and identification with		
--the middle class	65	35
--people of your race	61	28
--people of your nationality	54	28
--people of your religion	49	32
Men one admires		
--George Wallace	30	7
--Eugene McCarthy	24	65
Men one intensely dislikes		
--George Wallace	33	70
--Mayor Richard Daley	5	50
BASIC VALUES:		
Hard work keeps people from loafing and getting into trouble	54	18
Living the good Christian life defines success	75	36
Social changes that would be welcome		
--more emphasis on law and order	91	39
--more sexual freedom	19	48
Easily acceptable restraints imposed by society		
--prohibition against marijuana	77	37
--outward respectability for career's sake	54	17
--little decision-making power early in job	48	23
--abiding by laws you don't agree with	43	21
ABOUT BUSINESS		
Meaningful	49	23
Allows for self-development	42	16
Allows for creativity	37	13
Low ethics	23	48
Would not enjoy being involved with	17	46

However telling the above indices may be, the full measure of the polarization process and its calamitous impact on the nation's apparent state of dissension came to climactic expression in the realm of politics. Two significant examples may be cited:

(a) A first case in point was provided by the fact, as well as the effects, of the so-called "southern strategy" of the new Nixon Administration. This strategy both reflected and increased the soaring climate of resentment among the vast majority of America's lower- and middle-income whites, whose impressive electoral weight makes it into the single most important factor of the domestic political scene. For this reason, the current men in power could hardly be blamed for using all their political savvy in riding the groundswell of recalcitrance that had figured so greatly in their return to power. Yet there were signs that this savvy aimed less at weathering the storm by deftly steering toward calmer waters, than at letting the turbulent currents have their way--on the extremely risky assumption that, in the end, they would aid the helmsman's own purposes. On the one hand, there was a studiously upheld image of presidential aloofness that lent some credibility to Daniel Moynihan's (theoretically quite plausible) proposition that an aroused nation could benefit from a period of "benign neglect" of the major issues underlying the inflamed passions.[8] On the other hand, however, there was increasingly convincing evidence of a subtle policy of double-dealing that cynically exploited those very passions. Such evidence could be found in the glaring fact that the chief executive's prudence was but an ill-disguised facade behind which free rein was given to vice-presidential demagoguery and all sorts of similar appeals to backlashing constituents; while the ultimate effects came to light in the following, purely illustrative sample of cumulative developments that occurred within a period of a few months only (late 1969/early 1970), in the crucial and highly sensitive areas of Negro rights and justice-and-order:

--the Justice Department's promotion (as well as the approval of the House by a 208-203 margin) of a revision of the 1965 Voting Rights Act--a revision said to be aimed at a more equitable law but, in fact, eliminating the law's most effective core provisions that had enabled southern blacks to raise their number of registered voters by nearly 1 million and get six times more (from 78 to 463) officials elected;[9]

--the officially instigated drive against the Black Panther Party,[10] culminating in a nation-wide crackdown by means of rigorous prosecution and violent shoot-outs, and revealing an abysmal chasm of fear between a majority convinced of dealing with a deadly threat to the nation's security, on the one hand, and a minority equally convinced of being the ear-marked victims of systematically committed genocide, on the other.[11]

--the outrageous scenes of the Conspiracy Seven trial in Chicago (to which the Nixon Administration gave the green light, although the Johnson Administration had found insufficient reasons to do so)--scenes bearing out the "inevitable cause-and-effect relationship between repression and rebellion" (as Tom Hayden, one of the Seven, formulated it), and making devastatingly clear the total loss of faith, on either side, in the other party's integrity;[12]

--the bold attacks, encouraged by the administration's tactics of tacit endorsements, on whatever piecemeal progress had been made since the 1954 Supreme Court's ruling on school desegregation--as exemplified inside Congress by the Stennis and Whitten amendments aimed at further slowing down the pace of integration in obstructionist southern districts, and in the country at large by the growing obstinacy regarding even the most modest forms of token compliance with compulsory bussing programs.[13]

(b) In addition, reference can be made to the critical shockwave that rocked the nation in consequence of, or coinciding with, President Nixon's unilateral decision of late April, 1970, to extend the Vietnam war into Cambodia.[14] In this case, domestic discord not only exploded in horrible scenes of bloodshed triggered by the nervous over-reaction of law-enforcing authorities to various acts of frantic protest; but it also showed up in obvious signs of disaffection within the inner and outer circles of the establishment itself. Prominent members of the government's executive branch openly voiced their dissent; inside the legislative branch a raging battle developed, cutting across party-lines, to restore the proper constitutional balance in matters vital to national policy. And distinguished spokesmen of the country's academic elite, both white and black, arose as one man to express the utter outrage and frustration seething in their communities. To what significant degree the Cambodian gamble divided the nation's rank and file was disclosed by a swift poll conducted by Newsweek in the middle of May--the results of which intimated that for every five Americans in favor of the Cambodian operation, no less than four emphatically disapproved of it.[15] Yet on the other hand, this very poll suggested that, on the whole, the Administration's standing with the so-called "silent majority" remained substantially undamaged: 65 per cent indicated they were satisfied with the way the President handled his job in general; 84 per cent pinned major responsibility for the deaths at Kent State University on the student demonstrators; 60 per cent had no objection to the hard-hitting Agnew rhetoric about dissenters and protesters.[16]

Considering all this, it is hard to avoid the frightening conclusion that by 1970 the United States appeared to be rapidly approaching a condition of societal dichotomization. What seemed to be unfolding, at an ever-accelerating pace, was a complete breakdown of communication between bitterly opposed partisans who found themselves entrenched in fixed positions of mutual distrust and suspicion. Either side viewed the other as being beyond the reach of rational argumentation; and in this explosive atmosphere, each move that was made escalated the automatism of traumatic counter-moves--thus pushing the nation to a point where there seemed to be no future for a viable society.

The Vanishing Middle-Ground

In putting the above conclusion in such dramatic terms, we are fully aware of the risk of overstating our case. After all, the United States has experienced various periods of severe crisis in its history, out of which it has managed to emerge as a solid, resilient entity. Why then should it not succeed in weathering the new storm, the more so as the major forces of dissent were small in numbers and proved to be badly divided at that? Taken by themselves, these forces had no greater revolutionary power than to act as irritants. However, it is fairly evident that by the end of the decade they could not, and should not, be taken by themselves any longer; their function as irritants had produced effects that constituted incomparably greater perils to the nation's viability as a body politic than any actions of alleged or true revolutionaries combined. It was in the surging backlash of the counter-revolutionary multitudes that the erosion of America's deepest foundations loomed largest. In this backlash (rallying to the classic cry of law and order that traditionally has been the conditioned reflex of any society's resentment and insecurity when confronted with real or imaginary attacks on its established myths and mechanisms), the very essence of the American dream met its gravest threat. And this threat appeared to be of such virulence in recent years that we prefer to run the risk of overestimating its lurking consequences.

Besides, among these consequences there was one in particular which could hardly be described as merely lurking but, instead, posed itself as a problem of immediate concern: the impact the polarization process was having on American society's capacity to respond creatively, rather than repressively, to the transformative pressures of which the movement's radicalization during the late 1960's was a most significant indicator. It was the problem, in other words, of how one evaluated the odds this society was facing in its attempts to cope with the tensions that had been building up between those balking at change and those whose alienation incited them to seek change by any means.

Generally speaking, there were three major alternative courses that presented themselves, two of which were not necessarily mutually exclusive, since each could in effect become an extension of the other:

(1) resistance to change, at the risk of raising the level of forceful suppression to such a degree that for all practical purposes a police state would accrue;
(2) a full-fledged revolutionary blow-out, resulting in a violent overthrow of the old regime by a new one whose nature might vary from a system of reversed oppression to a vehicle of true transformation;
(3) pressure and counterpressure in striking a dialectic balance that would allow the society to be transformed along ultimately evolutionary lines.[17]

Viewing this problem against the background of the major trends as analyzed before, the odds were not encouraging. At the close of Chapter VI it was stated that by about 1970 it was by no means clear which direction the movement's transformative thrust was likely to take. The chances, however, that the "pragmatists" would have the upper hand appeared to be slim in light of the subsequent findings about the growing backlash among the nation's majority. For these findings implied two things which, put in terms of our multi-dimensional life-cycle model, read as follows: not only did it become quite apparent that life-cycle stage No. 3 now applied as well when seen from the $S \longrightarrow M$ perspective, but it became even more obvious that in this case the "breaking-point" strongly tended toward a preponderance of the "conservatives." And this, in turn, could well be read to augur ill for those who, within the movement and in the nation at large, sought to perform the tightrope act of pressing for radical change without arousing an extremism that would gravely jeopardize the achievement of such a change.

On the basis of these considerations, then, the prognosis could not but look grim indeed. It is a prognosis which plainly suggests that the larger society's response was such as to weigh heavily against any further progress on the part of the movement in successfully completing the final stages necessary for true emancipation.

LIFE-CYCLE STAGES, FROM THE S ⟶ M PERSPECTIVE

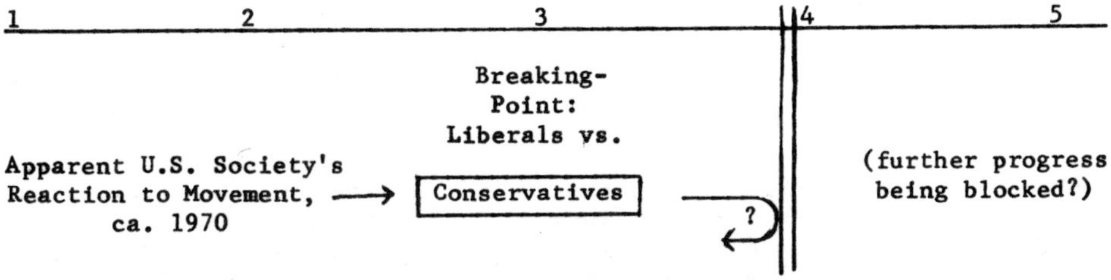

There is one factor, however, which has not yet been accounted for in the above prognosis; a factor of no small significance in determining the validity of that very prognosis. This factor consists of the state of mind of those who represent what might be termed the sociological category of the Middle-Ground.

By this category we mean approximately the same as "the intellectuals" whom Crane Brinton (in a context of great relevance to our present subject matter) roughly defines as "the writers, artists, musicians, actors, teachers, and preachers," who "are to a large degree committed by their function to take a critical attitude toward the daily routine of human affairs." It is especially the quality of functional role we would like to stress--and which prompts us to speak, in somewhat more specific terms, of a sociological category. This category, then, is made up of all those who carry the responsibility of shaping, giving expression to, transmitting, reflecting or commenting upon the flow of ideas that circulate within a given society. This responsibility places them in a peculiar sort of middle-position between the existing order of things and the norms inherent in ideas about what makes a social order just and good for its constituents. These ideas, as well as the norms derived from them, may differ widely; and so may their bearers and disseminators who, consequently, will vary greatly in the degree to which they consider themselves loyal adherents to established society. Nevertheless, all those shades and variations have one thing in common: in one way or another, they constitute the elements of a societal middle-ground, an indispensable buffer-zone between the forces bent upon an unreflected preservation of the past and those ready to blaze an equally unreflected trail toward a more or less chimeric future.

Having thus defined what we have labelled the category of the Middle-Ground, attention should be drawn to a particular section in

Crane Brinton's The Anatomy of Revolution, entitled "the transfer of allegiance of the intellectuals."[18] Such transfer, Brinton finds, on the basis of his studies, to be one of the significant symptoms, or "preliminary signs," of a society heading toward the outbreak of revolution. Its occurrence is marked by two developments:

(a) The emergence of substantially large numbers of intellectuals who find themselves in bitter opposition to existing institutions; an opposition which, in spite of all disagreements as to specifics, is united by a manifest desire for change. Putting it metaphorically, Brinton adds,

> we may compare intellectuals of this sort to the white corpuscles, guardians of the bloodstream; but there can be an excess of white corpuscles, and when this happens you have a pathological condition.

(b) The display of a qualitatively different attitude, partly resulting from the quantitative process just indicated, but above all indicating a definite turn from profound dislike for the way things are to enthusiasm for a "cause" spelling out the way things can and should be. It is this which marks the difference between the disaffection of alienated intellectuals and that of those who perceive a new vista, give birth to a new myth, and are consumed by a zeal to make the new world come true, here and now.

In applying his observations to the United States of the mid-1960's, Brinton was of the opinion that American intellectuals may be a protesting lot, but by no means were they inclined to transfer their allegiance.[19] To be sure, there was bitterness among them; yet as he saw it, this bitterness was not a sign of an impending revolutionary overturn, but rather represented the position that, traditionally, has been typical of intellectuals in American society. It is the position of people who think of themselves "as a class against other classes"--a feeling that stems from "a sense of being out of things in a country run by non-intellectual businessmen."

By the end of the 1960's, this opinion of Brinton seemed dated: the situation in 1965 was no longer that of 1970. On the basis of what our present study has attempted to show, it is obvious that too much had happened during this particular span of time. However, the extent to which Brinton's opinion was dated remains to be proved. And it is to this very task that we shall now turn.

There can be little doubt that the first of the two developments Crane Brinton considers characteristic symptoms of the actual transfer of allegiance was very much in evidence on the United States scene around 1970. This holds true not only for the intellectuals in a narrower sense, but also for the wider category of groups and/or subgroups we subsume under the term Middle-Ground. For several years it had been obvious that in broad circles of the intelligentsia per se, as well as in all sorts of institutions such as universities and churches, "the media," innumerable private and public research laboratories, planning agencies, and "think tanks," a vast number of voices had been raising a loud and consistent chorus of criticism. In addition, this chorus erupted in a dramatic climax following the events that accompanied President Nixon's Cambodian gamble in early May, 1970. This explosion demonstrated to what an alarming degree American society was exposed to fissionable material ready to blow up at any minute. A terrifying state of disintegration existed in the relationship between the nation's "thinking elite" and governmental authorities seeking to establish a "silent majority" rapport. Or to quote from the memoranda in which Alexander Heard, acting in his capacity as presidential campus adviser, issued grave warnings that, no doubt, also bore upon fields beyond that of his special assignment:

> . . . a national crisis confronts us. The condition cannot be conceived as a temporary, aberrational outburst by the young, or simply as a "campus crisis" or a "student crisis." Because of its immediate and potential consequences, the condition we face must be viewed as a national emergency.
> (Earlier,) many of us believed that deep disaffection afflicted only a small minority of students. Now we conclude that May triggered a vast pre-existing charge of pent-up frustration and dissatisfaction.

And to this Heard added:

> . . . self-identification by college students as a separate class in society is assuming extraordinary proportions . . . Some realist might well ask, whether the students, faculties, blacks and the others warrant all this energy and emphasis. They do . . . Power takes many forms in society. We are familiar with military power, financial power . . . Intellectual power ought not to be forgotten. Time and again in the world's history, ideas have prevailed over other forms of power, from the teachings of Jesus through those of Tom Paine . . . Intellectual power is at work in new ways in the United States.[20]

These conclusions and comments amounted in effect to saying that the first, quantitative condition underlying Crane Brinton's transfer of allegiance appeared to be all but fulfilled. In our judgment, this suggestion was a most persuasive one: what the country had been witnessing in the early summer months of 1970 could be likened to the sudden blaze-up of a long-smoldering subsurface fire that by this time had grown to ominous proportions. It is especially this latter quality which leads us to put such particular emphasis on the events of May 1970. However, these events differed in degree only from the many other instances that could be cited. A brief summary of such instances can be found in the following introductory remarks to a report of the mass arrests made during the "Mayday" demonstrations of 1971 in the nation's capital:

> A mass march on the Pentagon, Eugene McCarthy's Presidential campaign, banks burned, blood poured on draftboard files, peaceful rallies in the nation's Capital, a lethal bomb exploded outside a university research center--all these tactics, from benign to brutal, have been tried in efforts to speed the Vietnam war to an end. Last week, something new was added, both by the protesters and by the government they challenged. Antiwar militants mounted a display of aggressive civil disruption

in Washington's streets that strained the city's order, and the authorities responded with a wave of indiscriminate arrests and quasi-legal detention that warped the rule of law. The result was the largest mass arrest in United States history: 7,200 in a single day and a total of 13,400 during four days of gradually de-escalating confrontation.[21]

Yet the further suggestion implied in the conclusions and comments of the Heard memoranda--namely, that the second, qualitative condition was also rapidly materializing--strikes us as being a bit too rash.

To be sure, the intimation of a burgeoning intellectual power establishing itself as a political force over against the existing order could not be summarily dismissed. The question to be raised, however, was what direction this power was to take. Or to be more exact: what was its true quality, its dominant imperative? Was it that of acute disenchantment with the given state of affairs? Or did it have the makings of a concerted thrust that was pushing the cause of an alternative order?

In answering this question, we are strongly inclined to take the position that acute disenchantment constituted the predominant factor. Nowhere, in our reading of the facts, do we find sufficient evidence of a unifying principle that went beyond a raging disillusionment with the current reality. There is a lack of such evidence in the national crisis situation of which Alexander Heard spoke in his memoranda; nor do we find it--to cite another instance of crisis affecting Black America--in the reactions provoked by the December 1969 police raids on the Chicago and Los Angeles headquarters of the Panthers. At first sight perhaps, our view seems hardly warranted by the actual events. For in both cases, there was a massive rallying in support of the dissidents. It was a rallying, in other words, which not only lent credibility to the thesis of a manifest politicization of intellectual power but--even more significantly in terms of revolutionary potential--pointed to an emergent solidarity with a definite cause: the cause of the radicals of whatever class or color who opposed the present state of American society. Thus, following the brutal police-Panther confrontations, black and white leadership of impeccable credentials as regards "reasonableness," closed ranks in a furious outcry. This left little doubt as to the extent to which this particular minority's fate raised shocking questions about the American system's true margin of tolerance. In fact, the gnawing realization grew that this system--in spite of its much-tested excellence in upholding the constitutional rights of political deviants--proved capable of legalized persecution of the very victims of its own repressive reflexes. Similarly, the campus uprisings triggered by the Cambodia decision, with its gruesome aftermath of the Kent State killings, made it indubitably clear that the bitter protests once held to be the private preoccupation of an allegedly far-out fringe of activists, were now resounding in the utmost corners of every student hall, faculty room, and chancellor's office of the nation's citadels of learning. Or, to put it in the terse terms of a qualified observer, Kenneth Keniston, who was quoted in a mid-June 1970 survey on the explosive university scene: "The New Left is dead on campus. The positions it has maintained have been co-opted by liberals and moderates."[22]

Yet even in these distinct cases of across-the-board radicalization, the situation did not seem ripe for a decisive move to build another and better society. All that was apparent was an intensification of ill-feelings toward the established order among significant representatives of the Middle-Ground; but in neither case did this intensification show a clarification of objectives to which a new allegiance could be transferred. What prevailed instead was a sense of bafflement in the minds of those very moderates and liberals who, under the stress of circumstances, had been driven to radicalization.

The causes underlying this sense of bafflement we believe to be basically the following:

(a) In part, it was due to the radicals' apparent lack of precision in articulating their cause. Not even the foremost protagonists of a revolutionary reconstitution, whether black or white, succeeded in formulating an alternative vision of sufficient magic to turn feelings of outrage into mountain-moving acts of transformation. There was merely a glimpse of shimmering notions. It was a vision made up of basic humanist ideals but wanting in specifics as to how these ideals were to be translated into tangible counter-institutions that would work. As a matter of fact, there appeared to be a repugnance for all programs which reflected disgust with any question of structure or system. The matter of structure was too reminiscent of The System one abhorred. The result was that the revolutionary fire threatened to consume itself in an orgy of self-indulgences, ranging from bucolic communal bliss, to action-for-action's-sake, to violent anarchism.

(b) In part, the explanation for all this is to be found in the perplexities confronting those who, in the midst of a polarized society, feel they have to take sides yet would prefer to remain faithful to their middle-ground function of probing all a priori positions. These perplexities have been well summed up in the agonizing reflections of one life-long devotee to the cause of unconditional respect for any human being's integrity. Writing in 1968, this man, the late Francis O. Ayres, made an honest attempt at retracing the road he had gone and where it had led him.[23] What he found,

> . . . was that politically speaking, the middle ground was disappearing as a viable position. The sit-ins, the student unrest, the Vietnam War made a liberal stance impossible. One had to be a radical or admit that one was a conservative. After thirty years of comfortable, self-indulgent, middle-class liberalism this was a shaking of the foundations, which is exactly what was happening to the country as a whole.

Prodded by this painful discovery, he took to critically reassessing the concept of "revolution," as it had functioned from the eighteenth through the twentieth century. His investigations forced him to the haunting conclusion that, in contemporary America, revolution cannot be, and yet revolutionary action is imperative.

> On the one hand, I reject the idea of an all-out, across-the-board revolution. We are not dealing with Nicholas II, Chiang Kai-shek, Louis XVI, George II, or Batista. We have to deal

> with the most powerful establishment in history, controlling all the technical competence and backed by the overwhelming majority of the people. In addition, we have already gained most of what these other revolutions sought, or at least have been able to attain. Finally, no one has a coherent set of goals let alone a plan of how to attain them.
> Nevertheless, . . . there is much in affluent America, in the American Way of life, that represents a sickness. However, a full-fledged revolution would kill the patient. The totalitarian regime of the Right that would almost certainly follow an attempt at revolution would not be apt to help the poor and might well seek the final solution to the racial problem . . .

To this, then, he added, very much aware of the weak nature of his position:

> If on the one hand revolution in its classic form is out, revolutionary action is not. Any advance toward such goals as the eradication of poverty, racial justice, and an end to American imperialism will only come as a result of it . . . From the first sit-ins to the Resistance Movement, it has become increasingly clear that only revolutionary action will budge this country from its course.

(c) In the final analysis, however, these two explanatory factors point toward a more fundamental problem: the conditions underlying today's "technopolitan" society are such as to foil any attempt at formulating a clear-cut alternative. This society is the product of two sets of dominant forces that both enhance and frustrate human freedom.[24] It is a society in which man's struggle to gain control of his destiny (the principle of autonomy) is unsurpassed in its accomplishments. Precisely these accomplishments, however, call forth an intricate web of integrative mechanisms and regulatory procedures that are indispensable for maximizing this control (the principle of interdependence) but, at the same time, tend to strip the citizens of any significant voice in its exercise. In unleashing tremendous potentials of technological know-how and economic capacity, this society has created unprecedented opportunities for self-determination. Yet these very developments have given rise to an organizational superstructure of such unyielding complexity that full enjoyment of these opportunities is increasingly being thwarted. The net effect is that an eery climate of deadlock has been emerging, breeding apathy on the one hand (thereby strengthening even further the impact of organizational impositions), and angry protest on the other (growing the more rebellious the more the margins of meaningful participation are felt to be narrowing).

This deadlock can be broken only by a total commitment to radical humanization; but . . . what outlets are there for such a commitment which by definition entails the espousal of all-embracing, revolutionary changes in the present order of things? To stand a chance of success, demands for true transformation require a powerfully articulate projection of the New Order one envisions--if only to be sufficiently inspiring and concrete, to recruit the shock troops that can bring down the walls of resistance. However, such a projection is difficult to achieve since the established order professes the same set of ideals as the radicals--

liberty and equality. Therefore, the cause of the radicals remains indistinct, muddled and vague in the definition of what it is for. At best it amounts to lame generalizations. The result is that it lacks the necessary push to be effective. On the other hand, it may seek recourse in dangerously one-sided simplifications, by spelling out its objectives in terms of what it is against. In that case, the consequences may well be self-defeating. In view of the established order's power, as well as its complexity and inherent inflexibility, its built-in defensiveness against rocking-the-boat, there are awesome risks involved in an attack of any kind, but particularly if the attack is launched in the name of a cause that is largely negative. One such risk is that the assailants are likely to provoke, by their indiscriminate revolt, an equally indiscriminate mood of retaliation--thus precipitating a veritable trend toward totalitarian counter-revolution. Another risk is that the possibly ensuing battle will be fought with such uncompromising fierceness that it will be apt to end in the virtual destruction of those very foundations on which the actual realization of man's potentialities for self-expression has rested.

The Need of Moving Beyond the Dream

In summing up, the findings of the present study strongly suggest that by the end of the 1960's a situation had developed which can only be described as bleak. Anno 1970 was a time of acute polarization, confronting the nation with the spectre of a massive breakdown. To be sure, in itself (that is, in terms of our theoretical construct) this polarization process did not necessarily imply that such a breakdown would in fact occur; on the contrary, it might well indicate the imminence of a much more positive turn of events. As a specific stage of the Life-Cycle Model, polarization signals the approach of a breaking-point, which either marks a total breakdown, or a decisive breakthrough toward a new and substantially altered state of affairs. In view of our findings, however, there seems to be scant evidence that the United States in 1970 was about to move in the latter direction. The evidence rather suggests the reverse.

And yet today, now that a few years have passed, neither the breakdown nor the breakthrough can be said to have materialized. If there is any change, it is a change in the quality of the dynamics. Compared to the 1960's, when things were actively moving, the situation now seems to be one of passivity: things are being moved, anonymously; they drift. The once passionately engaged actors have lost their drive. They have given up, so it appears; not so much because they no longer care, but rather out of sheer exhaustion, if not total disillusionment. And this state of deadlock, of low tide, is mirrored by the society at large that seems to have grown apathetic to the pressures of change. These pressures have become so overpowering that they can no longer be responded to, but are eroding the capacity to react. To the extent that a condition of numbness prevails, those promising anything but change find no real match.

What does all this mean? That polarization does not exist any more? In our opinion, to draw such an inference would be a grave error. The process of polarization is still at work, for the underlying causes are still there. No conflicts have been resolved, no tensions have been relieved; rather they have deteriorated precisely because the basic ills within American society have not been alleviated.

Consequently, the conclusions which we have been forced to draw about the 1960's still seem to be pertinent to the present situation. However much we are aware of definite differences in the state of the movement as well as in that of the nation as a whole in 1973, or in the perspective of the 1960's, we believe that such differences do not really affect the substance of our conclusions.

These conclusions, then, read in brief review as follows:

--The movement, as it appeared by the end of the 1960's in both its two major composite strands of black revolt and white dissent, entailed a critique affecting the very roots of the American way and the inherited ideas, values and institutions that give substance to it;

--This critique had a deeply erosive impact on society as a whole, not merely by pitting an increasingly backlash-prone majority against violently disaffected minorities of various sorts and shades, but above all by fomenting a malaise, manifested in an appalling disarray of positions as to what is basically wrong with American society, and how it ought to re-order its priorities;

--Seriously adding to this all-pervasive malaise, but at the same time constituting perhaps the gravest symptom of it, was the harsh reality of the vanishing Middle-Ground, whose best representatives found themselves caught in a paralyzing dilemma: that of sharing the radical's intense feelings of alienation, yet seeing no viable alternative emerging from demands for total revolution, since such demands turn out to be as unspecified structurally as they are ideologically intransigent.

These three major conclusions lead to the agonizing question of whether the United States was then (and is today) nearing a breakdown for which there is no parallel in history. This is a shattering assessment, indeed. Yet it is not preposterous. For, in effect, the current situation (whether one writes 1970, or 1973) shows a number of unprecedented conditions in the nation's experience, including those most perilous moments during the bloody War between the States in the 1860's, or the Great Depression of the 1930's.[25]

Some of these conditions are, specifically: (a) Never before has America faced, as it does now, such a compounding of crucial problems--the problems of race, poverty, generational conflict, and a morale-wrecking war, together with their ugly ramifications of urban chaos, rampant fear, and general loss of allegiance--each single one of which poses a formidable challenge to the credibility of the American Experiment.

(b) Never before have the American people (in spite of the overwhelming Nixon majority of November 1972) been so estranged one from another, because of race, age, and class. So bitterly hostile are the countercultures that one may rightly wonder whether they possess the qualities upon which nationhood depends.

(c) Never before has such defection from America's sustaining faith in itself as a nation aspiring to moral perfectibility been so manifest. There are substantial segments of the population who are alienated--most notably the blacks, whose awakened will to assert their authentic "otherness" has dramatically exposed the dominant society's failure to grant identity on any terms save its own of white control.[26] In addition, there are the "turned-off" young, demonstrating an aversion to a system in which the triumph of technological achievement violates the worth of the individual. Lastly, there is the Middle-Ground, whose apparent state of paralysis reveals a critical impairment of the nation's regenerative powers to meet the staggering ills that afflict the present order.

Never before, in other words, has the United States met with a crisis so obviously striking at its very heart. It is a crisis which has culminated through the ravaging riptides of multiple change, in a crippling sense of shock. For what is at issue is the American dream, the concept of a new world that turns out to be an old world after all, an old world badly in need of fundamental transformations that go beyond a now deflated myth.

NOTES AND REFERENCES

Chapter VII

1. See p. 44.

2. "Characteristics of emancipation movements," J. A. A. van Doorn & C. J. Lammers, Moderne sociologie (Utrecht/Antwerpen: Aula Boeken, 1949), pp. 293-294.

3. In passing, it should be noted that the objection might be raised, whether the black liberation struggle and the white radicals' revolt can be discussed under the common denominator of an emancipation movement. Even though we believe to have demonstrated beyond doubt that both elements are inseparable parts of the U.S. Movement of the 1960's, one might ask whether there are no differences between the two, especially in terms of citizenship status. Without disputing the validity of this latter point, however, we would like to submit the following considerations: (1) Any emancipation movement is made up of those who, in the truest sense, suffer from being second-rate citizens, as well as those who, although enjoying full citizenship, identify with the underprivileged to the extent of joining their cause. (2) Yet even apart from this, there seems to be ample evidence that--despite obvious differences in objective citizenship conditions--black and white radicals alike view themselves as victims of the established order, since its structures and value system are viewed as denying them self-realization. (3) Besides, our definition of emancipation movements, as movements for change envisioning a new order, clearly applies to all component parts of the U.S. movement of the 1960's which, in consequence of its apparent radicalization, appeared to be fundamentally at odds with the dominant society.

4. White attitudes. Newsweek, issues of August 22, 1966, pp. 24-26 ("White Consensus: 'They're Trying to Go Too Fast,'") and October 6, 1969, pp. 20-38 ("The Troubled American: A Special Report on the White Majority").

5. Newsweek, August 21, 1967, pp. 18-19, ("After the Riots: A Survey").

6. Fortune, January 1969, pp. 70-71, 179-181 ("What They Believe").

7. The feelings and beliefs of the three-fifths non-dissident college students were found to be "remarkably similar to those of young men and women who have never attended college."

8. In itself, the Moynihan thesis was nothing but a variation on a general theme raised by many a columnist during the 1968 presidential campaign--to the effect that "moderates" like Humphrey, or "centrists" like Nixon, might be preferable candidates in order to ease the building tensions among the lower middle-class whites, due to the allegedly unrelenting push for controversial causes by the Kennedy and Johnson Administrations.

9. Newsweek, December 22, 1969, pp. 23-24 ("Voting Rights--or Wrongs?").

10. Newsweek, December 22, 1969, pp. 36-37 ("Too Late for the Panthers?"); Newsweek, February 23, 1970 ("The Panthers and the Law").

11. Perhaps the most morbid detail, evidence of the pathological quality of public phobia, was to be found in the Chicago Tribune's scoop on the bloody police raid on the Black Panthers' Illinois headquarters, in December 1969. In an "exclusive," this newspaper, the city's largest, unquestioningly swallowed the police account of killing-in-self-defense, as spoonfed by the Cook County State's Attorney's Office; included were "previously unpublished pictures purporting to show bullet holes in a door frame and a riddled door, evidence that the police came under withering fire." However: "A close examination of the scene showed that some 'bullet holes' were, in fact, nail heads. And the bullet-pocked 'bathroom door' in another picture turned out to be a bedroom door riddled by police fire." To which the Newsweek editor added: "Any newspaper can mix up an identification, but the Tribune's error seems not simply a product of carelessness but of a doctrinaire law-and-order stance that predisposes it to give uninspected credence to the police side of any story." Newsweek, December 22, 1969, pp. 62-63.

To add still another detail: in May 1970, that very spoonfeeding State's Attorney's Office was forced to drop its charges of murder and assault that had been brought against the 7 Panthers who had been taken alive during the raid. It was forced to do so . . . for lack of evidence. Newsweek, May 18, 1970, p. 28 ("Second Thoughts").

12. Newsweek, March 2, 1970, pp. 22-27 ("Judgment in Chicago"; "The Judicial Process on Trial").

13. Newsweek, March 2, 1970, pp. 18-21 ("Requiem for a Liberal Dream?"); Time, March 9, 1970, pp. 9-16.

14. Compared with the public outcry, then, the reactions within the U.S. to President Nixon's all-out bombing of Hanoi and Haiphong in December 1972 have been almost negligible. This difference is perhaps clearest evidence of the eery state of erosion suffered by the opposition forces today.

15. In contrast, public approval appeared to be considerably higher when, in 1965, President Johnson ordered air raids on North Vietnam (83 per cent) and dispatched U.S. troops to the Dominican Republic (69 per cent). Newsweek poll. Newsweek, May 25, 1970, p. 22.

16. It should be added, though, that in the last two cases the number of "no opinions" proved to be unusually high (respectively 31 and 24 per cent of the total sampling). Including the "no opinions" in the computation, the percentages in question would drop to 58 and 46.

17. The third course also may be labelled, in Saul Alinsky's terms, that of "orderly revolution." And as Alinsky reminds us, "To reject orderly revolution is to be hemmed in by two hellish alternatives: disorderly, sudden, stormy, bloody revolution, or a further deterioration of the mass foundation of democracy to the point of inevitable dictatorship." Saul Alinsky, Reveille for Radicals (New York: Vintage Books, 1969), p. 198.

18. Crane Brinton, The Anatomy of Revolution (New York: Vintage Books, 1965), Ch. 2/III.

19. It should be noted that the Brinton study we refer to is the expanded and revised edition of 1965.

20. Newsweek, August 3, 1970, p. 46.

21. Newsweek, May 17, 1971, pp. 24-29 ("The Biggest Bust: Washington Prevails Over the Protesters--At a Price").

22. Newsweek, June 15, 1970, pp. 46-51 ("Universities in Ferment").

23. Francis O. Ayres, at the time Episcopal chaplain at the Massachusetts Institute of Technology, in a paper for private circulation.

24. See Part One, Chapter III, "Autonomy and Interdependence."

25. It should be noted that, in this opinion, we are certainly not alone, but rather find strongly supportive evidence in the general tenor of the reflections of "six of the country's best-known historians . . . asked to assess the national spirit of '70 in the context of the whole American experience." It is doubtful whether this general tenor would strike a more optimistic note, if the question were raised today, in 1973. These historians (Andrew Hacker, Daniel Boorstin, Arthur Schlesinger Jr., Richard Hostadter, Staughton Lynd, and Eugene Genovese), although representing widely divergent backgrounds and points of view, definitely agreed "on the fundamental single point that America . . . is as profoundly under challenge as it has ever been." And at least three if not four of them went even further than that, by stating implicitly or explicitly that the present period is beyond parallel. Historians on "The Spirit of '70," Newsweek, July 6, 1970, pp. 15-30.

26. Black "otherness" and "turned-off" young. Gibson Winter, Being Free (New York: The Macmillan Company, 1970), esp. Chs. III-IV.

APPENDIX

ABOUT THE "GHETTO" CONCEPT IN THE UNITED STATES AND EUROPE

-- AN EXERCISE IN BECOMING AWARE OF ONE'S CULTURAL BIASES

The following pages tell of a personal experience of the author's as it was recorded by him during his stay with the Urban Training Center in Chicago, Illinois. There are three reasons for adding this piece of reflective reporting as an appendix to this study:

(1) In the first place, this experience relates to one of the central issues underlying our study of the movement. This issue concerns the fundamental question of how we, who stand in the century-old tradition of the so-called White Man's Burden, can break out of our (Western) cultural "ethnocentricity" which blinds us to an appreciation of the identity of others? The following narrative will deal with this question in a particular way. On the one hand, it will clearly demonstrate to what extent one's conceptualizations appear to be the product of the specific cultural and historic conditions in which one happens to find oneself. On the other hand, it will provide us with a clue to how one becomes aware of such a conceptual captivity.

(2) Furthermore, the report may be useful in explicating a general point which our study takes up in implicit terms only. It may bring home to the reader that what happens in the United States is by no means an exclusively American problem. It certainly is a European problem as well. Europeans may believe--rightly or wrongly--that they have rid themselves of the trauma of Jewish "otherness"; but this very trauma returns to them in the "otherness" of all sorts of immigrant groups from the world's economically underdeveloped countries, whose need for jobs serves to shore up the Grand National Products of the superindustrialized powers.

(3) Finally, the report may shed additional light on the phenomenon of the ghetto which--as has been described in Chapter VI--is of crucial significance in the struggle between "integrationists" and "separatists" of the Black Power brand. This very struggle is of global dimensions today. It affects the total world community and its future. On what terms shall this world community, for which there is no substitute if we are to survive at all, be built? On the terms of a white, Western civilization with which all other civilizations are supposed to be assimilated? Or on terms that will facilitate a transformation that will lead to a new, pluralist culture on a global scale, grounded in the distinct qualities of "other" identities, each one of which lays equal claim to (self) respect?

"Ghetto"--technically and more specifically defined

On arriving in the United States, some years ago, I was puzzled by the way in which the term "ghetto" was used in this country. As I understood it, the term was used here in a purely technical sense. It referred to the neighborhoods and attendant social, economic, political (in short: cultural) conditions of those groups not able or permitted fully to participate in the mainstream of American society. In other words, it applied to all minority groups generally, whether ethnic or racial, forced to live in a sub-standard environment as a result of not being accepted in, or not being acceptable to, the standards of the dominant social groups. However, the term applies only as long as these minority groups and/or their individual members have not succeeded in "making it" in the dominant society. Consequently, the implied assumption is (an assumption in keeping with the American image of "the land of opportunity") that in due course ghettos must--as some actually have--disappear thanks to the gradual passing of minority group members into the mainstream.

This struck me as being in fundamental contrast to the concept of "ghetto" which I brought with me from Europe. To me, familiar only with the phenomenon of the Jewish ghetto, the notion of eventual escape from it, or rather its eventual disappearance because its inhabitants had become members of the larger society, was completely inconceivable. As a European sociologist, I believed that the essential characteristic of the ghetto was precisely the *im*possibility of its minority to "make it" in the dominant society. *That* fact constituted the condition that made the ghetto what it was. Being a member of the ghetto was more or less the same as belonging to a "caste," a stratum of society completely sealed off from other strata.

Application of the double concept to the United States

In my opinion, therefore, the "real" concept of ghetto--that is, the concept as I had learned to understand it--applied in the United States to the ghetto institution only as experienced by the black (and other "colored") minorities in today's inner cities. For them it is, above all, a *compulsory* institution from which there is no escape because of the deeply entrenched discriminatory practices of the white majority in American society.

In a way, my biased approach (biased, indeed, even from a "scholarly" and/or European point of view, as I will indicate later) was an asset rather than a liability. It set me to thinking about possible explanations for the "loose" use of the term ghetto in the United States. Why--I asked myself--is the essential difference between the black ghetto as a racial institution and the earlier immigrant neighborhoods as ethnic concentrations not duly recognized or acknowledged?

Pondering this question, I began looking into a variety of earlier studies dealing with that typical American phenomenon of the nineteenth and early twentieth century: the immigrant communities in the large cities. What struck me--and this can only be a tentative conclusion--was that the term ghetto was virtually absent from these studies, unless one dealt specifically with the Jewish populations (as Louis Wirth did in his book, The Ghetto, published in 1928[1]). Yet, in more recent literature and in common parlance as well, it appears as though the black ghetto is viewed as a modern replica of the earlier immigrant quarters.

On the basis of this observation I submit--once again, tentatively --as a possible explanation, that the current use of the term ghetto, as applied both to today's black enclaves and yesterday's immigrant neighborhoods, reflects a hidden motive. I do not suggest that this is the result of a conscious construction. I am rather inclined to stress its unconscious nature. Nevertheless, the fact of the hidden motive remains; it mirrors the understandable tendency of this society--rhetorically and even actually committed to the American dream--to play down, to soft pedal, to think away, the crucial difference between the racial issue and the immigrant one.

It is a crucial difference, indeed. For if admitted, American society's deepest convictions of freedom and justice are shown to be applicable only to those who are not too different, and do not apply to those who put pluralism to a real test. To make such an admission is not easy, and I, for one, do not wish to sit in judgment. But this does not relieve us from the obligation of facing up to the unpleasant fact that a concept may be used for many different purposes, including concealing, rather than uncovering, an ugly reality.

Application to the European scene

To underline this point, I now hasten to add that my attempts to gain a fuller appreciation of the "ghetto" concept in the United States forced me to learn something about the European scene, as well. It became quite obvious that my understanding was conditioned by a much too limited perspective. Taking a closer look at the "ghetto" concept in its narrower, non-technical sense, and specifically dealing with the institution as experienced by Jews and blacks, the conclusion seems inescapable: even this narrowly defined concept appears to be the product of a hidden motive.

Historically speaking, the Jewish ghetto is, first of all, a "natural" phenomenon. That is, it originated as a voluntary institution, the product of a group seeing and experiencing itself as different from the surrounding society. Its aim was to protect its own identity and, at the same time, preserve this identity by furthering its own communal life. It is on this basis and for this reason that the earliest Jewish ghettos came into existence. Prior to the fourteenth century, the ghetto developed substantially through the autonomous action of the Jews themselves, without the pressure of outside forces, the population in general, or the authorities.[2]

It was only after 1300 that the voluntary ghetto was transformed into a compulsory one. At that point the general population together with the authorities deliberately began to set up social ghettos in order to eliminate or limit Jewish participation in commerce and handicraft. The final sanction for this type of segregation was given by Pope Paul IV in 1355, in his bull Cum Nimis Absurdum. This document was, in effect, merely a post factum theological rationalization serving the aspirations of the growing Christian bourgeoisie in obtaining wider municipal autonomy and commercial freedom from the feudal powers. The development of towns and their independent "burghers" produced a conflict with the princes whose best tax-payers had usually been the Jewish merchants. Members of Jewish communities, as non-Christians living their own separate cultural lives, had never been affected by church bans on the "evil" of interest rates and other matters incompatible with the rural, manorial order of the Middle Ages. As a result, Jewish merchants had achieved a virtual monopoly on trade. This monopoly now began to be challenged by the emerging commercial class of townsfolk.

Whatever these historic details--the rise of the ghetto as a compulsory institution, the product of very special socio-economic and political circumstances during a certain period in history, underlies the concept of the ghetto as it is generally used in European sociological terms. The question then should be asked: Why did this concept, in this particular sense, remain current up to the present? This is an intriguing question, indeed, considering two trends that have been developing for at least a century and a half.

(1) The first trend was one of the gradual disappearance of the compulsory ghetto as a legally instituted and enforced institution. With the French Revolution and the subsequent democratization of ever larger segments of European society, the Jews gained equal status de jure which they--in a manner similar to that employed by members of immigrant groups in the United States--often used as a means of escaping de facto from the ghetto and passing into the social mainstream;

(2) The second trend was that Jewish ghettos actually remained in existence, but on a voluntary basis. Many Jews simply did not wish to become part of the larger society but preferred to retain their distinct communal identity. There cannot be the slightest doubt (as will be shown) that more often than not this was a matter of their own free will, although one might ask to what extent this free will was at least in part conditioned by age-long compulsory segregation.

In other words, these two trends make it clear that the notion of inescapability, constituting the essential characteristic of the ghetto in its non-technical sense, no longer applied. Why, then, one may ask, had European sociology not taught me to revise the ghetto concept accordingly --that is, to include the voluntary type?

In reflecting upon this question, I came up with what I think are two major explanatory factors. The first is probably of minor importance, and yet for contemporary observers it carries great psychological weight. It is that of the reinstitution of the compulsory ghetto in its most abject form by the Nazis. Nobody who went through this experience, even as an outsider or non-Jew, can disassociate the term "ghetto" from the fate of the Jews in World War II.

The second factor is of a more fundamental nature. It has to do with a situation which seems to be analogous to that in the United States today, insofar as the race issue is concerned. This situation is that of the internal debate, if not struggle, within the Jewish community itself.

The liberal Jews, that is, those who sought to apply the theories of the French Revolution to the Jewish position in the modern state, did their utmost to destroy any remaining ghettos even of the voluntary type. To them, continuation of any form of (self-) segregation meant a weakening or even a threat to their assimilation or integration into the majority society. And to make this point as effective as possible they tended to speak and think of the ghetto in negative terms because of the hateful compulsory form of the institution. Since these liberal Jews were the ones with the most ready access to other intellectual members of the dominant society, their opinions did not fall on deaf ears.

On the other hand, the more conservative Jews, those who rejected assimilation and wanted to preserve their Jewish identity, resisted the break-up of the voluntary ghetto in which they were comfortable and best able to perpetuate group solidarity (as well as their own traditional position of leadership). Around 1900 and later, these conservative Jews found powerful allies in the Jewish nationalists, or Zionists, who--in contrast to the assimilative liberals--tended to place great emphasis on the positive values of the ghetto for the Jewish community. These nationalists demanded the opportunity for an autonomous group life, which internal conditions within the ghetto provided in no small measure; for through the ages this ghetto had developed a closely knit communal organization (with a wealth of indigenous institutions), a strong sense of religious-racial-national solidarity, plus a cultural life with definite characteristics of its own.

Conclusion

This debate between Jewish liberals and nationalists and their respective conceptualizations of the ghetto seems to have a contemporary ring for us, who today witness a similar struggle in the United States, particularly in the black community. Everybody can draw the parallel for himself. I would like to add two final comments:

(1) The debate highlights the same basic dilemma which nowadays confronts those in the black community who take the "integrationist" or the "separatist" position. In both cases the dilemma is:

--How can a long segregated minority ever achieve acceptance in a majority society unless it destroys the conditions which reflect its separateness from that society?

--Yet, how can a minority group ever hope to exert effective pressure on the majority society to force it to acknowledge the minority's right to self-expression and self-determination unless it nurtures and preserves the conditions from which solidarity and awareness of one's identity emerged?

(2) This dilemma may seem as applicable to the Jewish as to the black communities, but, in fact, the analogy cannot be carried all the way. There are two important reasons for this. First, the black ghetto is now not a voluntary but very much a compulsory one, if not de jure, at least de facto--a ghetto in the "caste"-type sense. Secondly, the black ghetto does not usually have the internal cohesion the Jewish ghetto had (or has). It is certainly not at present a well-knit social and cultural web of communal organizations; nor is it marked by a strong and sharply articulated sense of religious-racial-national solidarity. All it does have is the distinct characteristic of what Oscar Lewis has termed "the culture of poverty."[3] It is precisely in search of a cohesion that transcends poverty that the themes of "Black unity" and "Black control of the ghetto" are raised today. However, whether such unity and control are possible, is in no small measure dependent on whether the ghetto is a voluntary or a compulsory one. And this is the dilemma we face today, as plainly as ever.

NOTES AND REFERENCES

Appendix

1. Louis Wirth, The Ghetto (original edition, Chicago: University of Chicago Press, 1928).

2. There are clear parallels here with the function of the ethnic immigrant quarters in 19th and early-20th century America, as well as that of the separatist organizations of "confessional" minorities, such as the Roman Catholics in Holland.

3. Oscar Lewis, La Vida (New York: Random House, 1966), pp. xlii-lii.

NOTES ABOUT THE AUTHOR . . .

Paul E. Kraemer is currently director of the research division of the Interuniversity Institute for Value Research and Training in Rotterdam, The Netherlands. Previously he has served as member and subsequently as associate director of the Sociological Institute of the Reformed Church in The Netherlands. He was the director of research at the Urban Training Center for Christian Mission, Chicago, Illinois from 1965-1969. Among other activities, he has also been a visiting lecturer in the Ethics and Society Field of the University of Chicago and has served as co-editor of Sociologisch Bulletin. He is the author of Gemeente In Meervoud (Congregations in Multiple Situations), The Societal State, Rebels With A Cause and Chicago Journaal (in Dutch).

Dr. Kraemer was educated at the University of Leiden and the University of Michigan. He received his Ph.D. in the Social Sciences from the University of Leiden.

He is presently living in Bilthoven, The Netherlands. He is married and has three children.